CW00923262

SIRIUS

Geoffrey Bingham grew up on Sydney's North Shore. He served in Malaya with the AIF, won the Military Medal for bravery in the field and later was a prisoner-of-war in Changi and elsewhere. Always interested in writing, he found his short stories eagerly accepted by the *Bulletin* and other periodicals upon his return to Australia. After five years of farming and writing he "got down to the business of his life" — theology — and writing was put aside. He became a minister of the Church of England and for over 25 years worked for the Church in Australia and all over the world. Now, settled in Coromandel, South Australia, where he has his own publishing company for theological books, he has come back again not only to Australia, but to writing. The stories in this collection are mainly from his *Bulletin* days. As Douglas Stewart notes in the Foreword: "Geoffrey Bingham's stories have improved and matured; and it is all the better to have them gathered together in book form, where we can see what his world is made of and feel its full impact."

TO COMMAND THE CATS

and other stories

With a Foreword by
Douglas Stewart

GEOFF BINGHAM

PUBLISHED BY ANGUS & ROBERTSON

Published with the assistance of the Literature Board of the Australia Council.

ANGUS & ROBERTSON PUBLISHERS
London • Sydney • Melbourne • Singapore
Manila

First published by Angus & Robertson Publishers, Australia, 1980

© Geoffrey Bingham 1980

National Library of Australia
Cataloguing-in-publication data.

Bingham, Geoffrey.
To command the cats.

(Sirius quality paperbacks)
ISBN 0 207 14226 2
ISBN 0 207 14218 1 Paperback.

I. Title. (Series).

A823'.3

Printed in Hong Kong

*For Douglas Stewart, and the memories
of his encouragement.*

ACKNOWLEDGEMENTS

Acknowledgement is gratefully made to the *Bulletin* for permission to use "Laughing Gunner", "The Cat and the Clown", "Killa T'Pig, George", "The Mind of Matsuoko", "To Command the Cats", "Mr Hicken's Pears", "The Sons of Nim", "Private Amnig, V.C.", "The Little Oak", "Dolly", "Grandma Sells Persimmons", "Tallyho the Red Rascal", "The Inspector" (originally published in longer form as "Need a Wife") and "A Bid for Beauty"; and to *Southerly* for permission to use "Concerning Grass".

CONTENTS

FOREWORD

For more than quarter of a century Geoffrey Bingham has been invisible to mortal eye, at any rate in the Sydney literary world, and I for one am very glad to see his reappearance in this book.

Back in the late 1940s, when I was on the *Bulletin* staff, he made a reputation in that paper for short stories of two widely differing kinds. One was a set of pictures of World War II in Malaya, where Geoffrey Bingham had served with the AIF, won the Military Medal for bravery in the field, and afterwards been a prisoner-of-war in Changi and elsewhere. The second group of stories was about country life in New South Wales, mostly at a place he called Wirril Creek.

The *Bulletin* management liked one of the Malayan stories, ''Laughing Gunner'', so much that they advertised it on our posters all round the town — and indeed all round Australia — as our main attraction for the week: a most gratifying episode to those of us on the literary side of the paper, for it wasn't often that our unworldly concerns achieved such prominence. ''Laughing Gunner'' was about a lone machine-gunner crouching exultingly over his weapon as the Japanese tide poured over him; and, like a number of Geoffrey Bingham's other stories, was concerned with the kind of soldiers who, whether alone or in a massed charge, found themselves fulfilled in war . . . a strange phenomenon to contemplate, as Geoffrey Bingham himself says, in the after-days of peace.

The Wirril Creek sketches, which followed the Malayan stories, or perhaps were mingled with them, were necessarily lighter in tone. They had affinities with the comedies of the earth which such admirable writers as Brian James and E.O.

Schlunke were publishing in the *Bulletin* at that time, but had an odd, elusive charm of their own, almost a touch of fairytale, as if, after Changi, Geoffrey Bingham was seeing the Australian countryside as Arcady; which I suppose it was. The persimmons ripened in the sun; and Grandma, though she could be tough enough with tourists she didn't like, let the Aboriginal boy help himself to as many as he could cart away.

Then, after five years of farming and writing at Eungai Creek on the north coast and Woodhill on the south coast, Geoffrey Bingham decided to become a clergyman. It wasn't a sudden decision, for he had entered Moore Theological College in Sydney just before the war; but it was, nevertheless, surprising. I remember him bounding into the *Bulletin* office one day to tell me about it — young, full of sturdy vigour as he was then, his blue eyes alight with enthusiasm.

He vanished.

Where he vanished to, as I now learn, was into a most interesting and adventurous career in the Church of England. He was Rector of the Sydney Garrison Church for four years; then off to Pakistan (where he was founder and principal of the Pakistan Bible Institute), India, Ceylon, North Borneo, Malaysia, Thailand, Hong Kong, Japan, the Philippines, Indonesia, New Guinea, England, the U.S.A., and New Zealand.

Now, settled in Coromandel, South Australia, where he has his own publishing company for theological books, he has come back again not only to Australia but to writing. He has written ''a sort of fantasy'' and a novel, has plans for other books, and in the meantime has put together the present collection of short stories. It consists mostly of his *Bulletin* stories, with a few others that I haven't seen before, such as that tense, macabre, altogether remarkable story ''The Mind of Matsuoko''.

How have his stories got on, during all these years of waiting? It is a curious fact that writing lying in store — or on the shelf, for that matter — never stays still. As one of the philosophers said about Man himself, it moves continually towards its increase or its decrease. It improves or it deteriorates. It matures or it gets corked.

In my opinion Geoffrey Bingham's stories have improved and

matured; and it is all the better to have them gathered together in book form, where we can see what his world is made of and feel its full impact.

Douglas Stewart

LAUGHING
GUNNER

They began calling him "Tiger" after a while. Not that there was any reason for it. Alan started it: "He's a tiger," said Alan, "a tiger with the thing."

He was, too, but the word "tiger" in that context is slang. Not that we didn't use slang — we did. Even the kid called Tiger used it, but it was not often he spoke.

He was queer that way. In the Army you find it hard enough to stop some chaps talking. They want to go on and on, and it means putting a drink into them, or, if they're sick, a thermometer. No, they won't stop, and it's no use giving them a drink either, when you think it over, because they only talk a lot more. Young Tiger didn't talk very much.

To look at him you'd think he'd do a lot of talking. He was a good-looking kid in his own way, and one you'd think the girls would fall for, but you'd be wrong. They shied away from him, as though maybe there was something funny about him. When you thought about it, too, there was something funny about him. He didn't like people, and they didn't cotton to him, not quickly anyway.

I liked him, but maybe I like most people; I don't know. I liked Tiger because there was something about him I admired. Men don't like a fellow who keeps to himself, but Tiger was so young that they thought he shouldn't be in the Army, and that would excuse any faults he had. It wasn't as though Tiger worried very much about any thoughts they had about him. He was just self-sufficient, I suppose.

1

Sometimes I would catch him looking at someone, and there would be a strange gleam in his eyes. I don't rightly know what it meant. Even now I don't know what it meant, but then it's hard to know these things.

"If he wants to be left alone," said Alan, "then leave him alone."

"I think we should pal up with him a bit," Jon said; but after a while they all left him alone. They stopped saying things to him, too.

At first they used to gig him on his parade-ground work. He just couldn't march. Put him with a column of men and you would see his legs moving against the easy swing of the platoon. Everyone in step except Tiger, and he walked along sublimely ignorant of the error of his step. Men hated marching behind him, because they trod on his heels; or in front of him, because he trod on theirs. To see him with a rifle would make you groan. Clumsy and awkward it was in his hands, and it sent a shiver through you to see him slope arms or order arms or present arms. Officers and non-commissioned officers tore their hair trying to show him how to do it, but with no avail. He just plugged along — go your way, I'll go my way — and what could you do about it? Everyone gave up trying.

They would keep him off the big parades — you know, where you present arms to a big shot with brass around his hat. Yes, they were careful to keep him off those, and yet I have seen sergeant-majors nearly go mad when at the last moment he would wander on to the parade-ground, a vacant look on his face, and his rifle trailing behind him, and maybe a puttee trailing, too, and his buttons all undone.

In his eyes there would be an empty look, and his face would be devoid of expression. He comprehended none of our urgent gestures. The sergeant-major would look at him with agonised expression, and in a painful whisper would mutter, "Get him off quickly, quickly. I'll go mad if he doesn't. I'll kill him, that's what I'll do. I'll kill him." Someone would race over to Tiger and lead him away. It seemed a pity, but there it was.

You'd say he was no good for anything, and at that time you wouldn't have been wrong. It was only when we started on machine-gun work that the change came.

You should have seen that boy on the machine-guns. It was uncanny the way he picked up knowledge about them. Any kind of machine-gun or sub-machine-gun. He liked the Vickers the best.

When the lectures started he was there first. He never turned up late for m.g. classes. He was first with the answers, too. Knew everything there was to know about rates of fire and lines and fields of fire, and how many parts there were to a Lewis, and he could disassemble and reassemble with his eyes closed, and beat even the experts. Yes, he was a ''tiger'' on them, as Alan said.

If the lecturer asked about enfilading fire and effective ranges, and questions like that, then the class could sit back and listen to Tiger. He knew. He seemed to be in his element. The rest of us he did not see. We did not count. It was the machine-gun he liked. His hand would creep over it in a caressing way.

''That kid ain't natural,'' Alan whispered to me.

I muttered something about no soldier being natural, but he was right. There was something strange about this young fellow. I learned to become proficient with machine-guns, but even now they don't thrill me; most of us were like that.

When we went on board the transport that took us to Malaya the platoon sergeants were busy giving the men their bayonet drill, and you could see and hear them trying to work up the troops.

''Point!'' they would yell in a loud voice. ''Withdraw!'' they would scream, and then in a fury, ''Point! Withdraw! Point! Withdraw!'' and the men would be nearly mad with imagination, and the bayonets would be flashing. And yet Tiger did not like the bayonet any more than he liked the rifle. It was queer when you came to think of it. In the end they left him with his machine-guns, and if you went up on to the top deck you would see him there day and night, staring over the sight. At night when the moon came out you could see him, white and pale, as he searched for aircraft.

The sergeant who wanted him to point and withdraw was disgusted at Tiger's unseeing indifference. "Hell!" he would say. "Call that a soldier!"

"You should see him on the Vickers," said Jon, and after that the sergeant left him alone. They forgot all about him when we drew into Singapore.

Later, when the war broke out, they remembered him. They put him on a Vickers right down on the Mersing Beach. The chaps in that show remember how open the beach was to attack, and how Tiger fired, laughing, at a Jap aeroplane that came swooping towards the yellow sand. The aeroplane dived angrily at him, but he only laughed and kept firing. When the bomb landed near him he went further along the beach and still kept firing.

After that show we went to Singapore Island. Things were grim there, much different from the east coast, and all day long the great ack-acks thumped away at the sky. We were short of planes there. The Japs had plenty, and they bombed our positions on the north-west sector of the island, and across the Straits of Johore boomed about five hundred field guns, and they landed one quarter of a million shells in our sector in just about twenty-four hours. Still we crouched in our weapon pits and m.g. nests, and we waited. We knew they would come, and in the end they did come.

They came on Sunday night. The yellow men tumbled from their armoured barges into the water. The water was dark with their dead. Our guns hammered loudly, in a kind of mad song. Sometimes we'd hear one stutter, somewhere out in front of us, and go quiet.

Jon and Alan and I crouched over ours. We had tommy-guns over our shoulders so that we could be ready if the guns jammed. Tiger was close to the water, and we could hear his gun and then the others came through, those who had run their guns hot or jammed them. Nodding as they passed us, they left us bent over our guns. There was no glory in their eyes, and they seemed weary to death. Tiger had come back with them,

4

and now his gun was in an empty pit near ours. Then the enemy came through.

They had their old stunts of throwing crackers, and screaming, but we were ready for that. Tiger's gun crackled first, and it became the joyful thrumming of a song of death. The Vickers raked the long lalang and the barbs that twirled and twisted through the short rough scrub. The hillocks were kept clear of the enemy. They jammed up against the wire. They writhed in the now grey grass.

We were tired with weaving bandoliers into the guns, and snapping new magazines into the Bren. The guns became hot. Someone had a tommy-gun going, and it was doing good work even at its range. Then our gun jammed, and in the heat of it all we could do nothing.

"We'll have to get out of it," yelled Jon, and he grabbed his rifle. He picked up a lump of iron and smashed into the gun. After that we went quickly because there was a hail of fire near us. Alan, who had the Bren, fell and I grabbed him. Jon cursed in a terrible voice, but it was no good. He was done for.

Only after we got away a bit did we hear the other gun still singing, and Jon said, "Good God! That's Tiger."

I said, "Maybe it's just Tiger. I don't know about the crew." And we were silent.

"He's a fool!" Jon said, and we both knew that, but didn't like to think about it at all.

We heard the gun for some time, and then things got hot again, and we lost the sound of it. Jon and I spent the night on the aerodrome. We had a tin of bully-beef between us.

Next morning we saw Tiger. He just stared at us. Our gun jammed, we told him. He just nodded. "I knew that," he said; nothing more.

Jack, who had been with him, told us the other men had been killed and Tiger had told him to go if he wanted to. They had plenty of ammunition, and Tiger was prepared to stay. Mad but brave. The enemy had swung about on their flank, and although things were pretty thick they had managed to get away.

"Nearly too late," Jack had said; and then, softly to us,

''He's mad!''

On the Wednesday night the enemy came through and cut off our company. We did not know until suddenly we heard their crackers and cries and realised they were on our right flank.

We wondered if they would swing across our front and then push us round. They didn't, but then we heard them on our left flank, and we knew that was the end. Jon and I looked at each other and we were pretty sick, and then after a moment or so one of the reinforcements we had on our gun just turned over and groaned. He was dead.

The other chap said, ''They'll get us.''

''So what!'' said Jon savagely. ''What if they do?''

The reinforcement said nothing, but looked unhappy. Then Tiger's gun began to hammer, and we knew they were there. We set ours going, too, so that the two guns were singing a twin song, a rising and falling song which had the tone of madness through it, a sort of divine ecstacy, a fearful joy. I heard it most in the song of Tiger's gun, and I shivered, knowing I would never forget it.

The rounds were heating the gun, and I was praying the heat wouldn't seize it. It didn't. If it had we would have had to leave Tiger and his gun alone, and we knew what that meant. It was all or nothing here, and no soldier wants to die. He wants to fight maybe, but not to die.

Tiger had two men on the gun with him, but only one was in our view. A moment later and he was over to us, reporting progress. We saw him crawling through the grass, and then his sharp excited tones told us all. The other chap was killed and Tiger wanted more ammo; it was madness for us both to stay there. It needed only one gun on this short front; maybe we could get through. Tiger wanted to stay, and our ammo would do him; we'd better move pretty quick.

Jon took the gun, and I looked across to where Tiger was. There was a red glow from some fire or other, maybe a burning dump, and I could see his face. It was set with an intense joy such as I have never seen on any man's face. He was staring ahead with the pale red light flickering up into the set hollows of his cheeks. The gun in his hands was singing the joy of the man.

Involuntarily I shuddered at this terrible magnificence. No awkwardness now; no blundering on to parades and being taken off. His life had reached some wild climax. He was a god, laughing, seized with the divine madness of death.

I gave ammo to the gunner, and he went across with it to the pit. I saw him crawl through the grass, and then I turned to Jon. "He'll stay there," I said. "He'll stay there till crack of doom. We'd better get out!"

"Maybe that's being a coward," said Jon, and it was hard to read his voice.

"Maybe," I said, "but he'll stay there even if we don't and he wants us to go. There's only ammo for one gun now."

"I see," said Jon, and his hand was still on the trigger. For a moment, which might have been years, I looked across at the man who had been a misfit. Then he had seemed but a boy, but now he was full with his years and the glory was through his face. With each rise and fall of the mad song of his gun his joy pulsed through him.

"Look," I said to Jon, and he let the gun go, looking at him.

"God!" he said sharply, and then the other gunner was across to us again.

"He said to go," he whispered excitedly. "He's mad. So are we if we stay."

"We'll go," said Jon quickly, and with pain in his voice. "Get the gun quickly," he said, and we made ready to go. Somehow I got the ammo and ran across to where Tiger was. The air was thick with bullets, and I laughed at that because the madness of the boy reached out to where I was and drew me with it. Jon and the other two I could see moving through the trees. I threw the ammo into the weapon pit, and he said "Good!" in an exultant voice, and without turning his head.

"Luck!" I said to him, and knew that was a mad thing to say, and not effectual. He took no notice, and when I went through the trees I could see the madness laughing from his face, and leaping from the gun.

7

Looking back I saw the smile on his face, and then I had to run because thousands of the enemy were coming, and the night was filled with shots and cries.

THE CAT
AND
THE CLOWN

All were skinny, but some were long and skinny, as was Ray.
He looked down at the English colonel, and the English colonel
looked up at him.

"Jugged cats," said the colonel, and he began to laugh.

"I've heard of jugged hare, sir," Ray ventured politely.

"Heard of it!" said the colonel, amazed. Then he stared at
Ray, his blue eyes becoming keen. "You were at Kamburi,
weren't you?" he asked.

Ray nodded. "No jugged cats there, eh?" the colonel
shouted.

The tall Australian was mystified. "No, sir," he said
wonderingly.

"Look," commanded the colonel. "Cats! Cats everywhere!
Damn foolish Indians lived in this camp before." He gestured,
embracing in the one movement of his arms the entire
prison-camp. "Never eat cats, apparently," he said soberly.

Ray drifted away from the English colonel. He remembered
him now, doggedly retaining his pack on the long trek in
Thailand. Very red in the face, the colonel had been. Probably
dreaming of jugged hare.

The cats were thin, but they were very trusting. Too trusting.
The colonel and others lost little dignity in catching them.
Three days in the ground, the cooler the spot the better, and
then cook 'em. The colonel and his friend, if they did not fatten,
at least felt some satisfaction, and undoubtedly they discussed
the dish in epicurean manner.

"Puss, puss, puss." They had formerly been spoken to in Hindustani or Nepalese, or something, but they responded to "Puss, puss, puss," as though the words were universal, and they universal cats.

The Yanks greatly rejoiced as the cats grew scarcer. Hank especially. He and his fellow soldiers reasoned that a benign Providence works in wondrous ways. When cats are gone — and who does not like a cat? — then the rats will come. Hank, the musical Yank, offered one dollar — in Japanese currency, of course — for a rat, small or big.

Hank had even offered Ray a bite, big Ray who would rather be thin than have cats or rats on his conscience and in his stomach.

"But you see," Hank explained, "it's all done by science. When it's titivated and done up it might be anything."

"No," Ray said gloomily. "I'm hungry, but I'm not starving."

"Some people," said Hank, "never know when they're starving."

"A good thing," Ray observed.

"If you had a cat now," said Hank, intending to be cruel, "what would you do with it?"

"Nothing," said Ray truthfully.

Hank would not believe that. "A whole big cat?" he asked incredulously.

"A whole big cat," Ray maintained.

"But you would get nine dollars for it," Hank said.

"Very very nice, too," said Ray. "But all the cats are gone."

"All gone," agreed Hank wistfully. "But there are the rats." His eyes brightened. "They'll come. They're bound to. They can fatten on soap. Soap's fattening."

"You can't eat soap," said Ray sadly.

"I'm not so sure," Hank said.

And then it was Ray saw the kitten. At least it seemed to him to be a kitten, but probably it was a small cat. It parted the leaves of some tapioca plants and peered out. It was probably, Ray thought, the last cat. The cat, too, might have thought so. It stared at Ray, without suspicion, but long and seriously. It withdrew slightly when another prisoner came to where Ray was.

"A cat," he observed. "I wish I had time to catch it." He looked at Ray enviously. "Lucky," he said.

"Time?" said Ray. "Haven't you plenty of time?"

"I have to go to the Nips' cookhouse and cut wood," the prisoner-of-war said, licking his lips. It paid to cut wood at the Nips' cookhouse.

"You could do it easily," he told Ray out of the corner of his mouth. "If you watch Yostler."

"Why watch Yostler?" Ray asked.

The other soldier began to laugh softly, as though he, too, knew the joke, but appreciated Ray's gesture of humour.

"Old Yostler, eh?" he said with rare good humour as he departed.

What has Yostler to do with it? The tall Australian wondered. The kitten emerged again, and he saw it was not small or thin, a remarkable state of affairs.

"Kitty, kitty," he said, almost automatically.

The kitten looked at him. The last cat, or kitten, it longed, seemingly, for company.

"Kitty! Kitty!" Ray said.

And archly it came, back curled sinuously, eyes voluptuous, tail moving slowly, an innocently-wicked enchantress.

"Meow!" It was a faint sound, but a sweet response.

"Oh, kitty, kitty, kitty!" said Ray soothingly, foolishly.

Kitty seemed to know it was all in order to be stroked. She rubbed her smooth softness against his skinny leg. She caressed with her silky fur the nobble of his ankle. She liked his fingers moving along her back. She looked up and flirted gently.

"Kitty," he crooned.

Then he remembered; watch Yostler. Kitty continued to smooge, even when he lifted the chunkel in businesslike manner, tilling the ground.

"You would be very tender," he told her reprovingly.

11

Nine dollars, Hank had said. Nine dollars. It was like selling your soul. Yet not to sell would be madness. Poor little Kitty. He spared a moment to stroke her.

"Go away, Kitty," he warned. "Go away! Shoo!"

Kitty was most coy. She arched her back in friendly manner. She refused the warning.

"I'll be glad," said Ray desperately, "when the gong goes."

After a time the gong did go, echoing across the camp, but Kitty did not go. Nor did she stay. She followed the tall Australian across the freshly tilled soil. Both she and the prisoner had no premonition of what was to follow.

He suddenly picked up Kitty and placed her in his shirt. She nestled there, still purring. She was exquisitely soft against his ribs. Perhaps she had gone to sleep. He hoped so when he saluted Yostler. Yostler did not seem to see him. He was smoking a delicious cheroot and was, consequently, dreamy. Possibly thinking of geisha-girls.

It was inevitable Hank should turn up from somewhere. Hank, living in the same camp, was bound to strike up against you. Hank, with his uncanny gift for smelling out the unusual; but even then Ray had no thought of connecting Hank, Kitty and nine dollars. Yet some impulse prompted him to withdraw Kitty from his shirt.

Kitty awoke. She stared up at Ray, then, almost arrogantly, at Hank. She yawned impolitely.

"Ray," said Hank earnestly, "I thought you were only a child in these things. I'll admit defeat."

"Oh," said Ray.

"That," said Hank ungrudgingly, "is the best cat I've set eyes on ever, bar none."

"It's a nice cat," Ray said.

"Worth five dollars any day," said Hank.

"You said nine this morning," said Ray, remembering.

"Ha," said Hank. He stared suspiciously at Ray.

"And if this is a better cat than you've seen. . . ." Ray said.

Hank looked at him, "I used to think you were a chicken," he said, "or a clown."

"Well!" Ray said indignantly.

12

"Kitty, kitty, kitty," Hank said hungrily.

Then his eyes widened. "That," he said, "is Yostler's cat."

"No!" Ray said.

"Nestles up on his bed every night," said Hank. "Yostler loves that cat."

"Well!" said Ray a second time.

"Poor old Yostler," commiserated Hank. "And he's the best of the bunch, too, though that ain't particularly difficult."

"Fancy," said Ray. "Yostler's cat, eh?"

"Well, now," said Hank in a businesslike manner. "If you came in on this cat we could pay you so much, and you could take the rest out in cat and vegetables."

"Vegetables?" said Ray.

"Paw-paw, cooked green. A little tapioca." He stared solemnly at the Australian. "And," he added powerfully, "some towgay."

"Oh!" said Ray.

"Say five dollars without the meal, three with it," Hank suggested.

"You wouldn't kill Kitty!" said Ray.

"You are a clown," said Hank. "I love some of your jokes. Now what about the price?"

Ray looked down at Kitty, up at Hank. "A little thing like that." Then he added hastily. "Plump, of course."

"Yostler was a good master," said Hank.

"Yostler," said Ray slowly, and he was decided. "Ten dollars or nothing," he said firmly. Hunger gnawed at him, too, as it had at Hank, as it had at all the poor pussies with the exception of Yostler's pussy. Also Yostler was very fat, and smoked cheroots. There were cheroots in the canteen, though highly priced. Still, with ten dollars . . . .

"Aussie!" said Hank in a pained voice.

"Listen," said Ray firmly. "One cat, ten dollars. No vegies, see? No food. Ten dollars. I want cheroots."

"Now, look here," said Hank.

"Ten dollars," Ray said. He began to see now the whole plan, the wide merriment of the English colonel, Hank laughing at him, Kitty carelessly appearing from the tapioca, Yostler ignorantly happy in his own world and soon to lose his lover, and he, Ray, soon to calm his edged nerves on the cool sweet flow of cheroot smoke. It was all very wonderful.

"Ten dollars, then," said Hank, and he stared curiously at the Australian. "I can't make you out, Ray," he complained. "Still, when you're hungry you'll do anything."

"So you will," agreed Ray. "Anything," he added, and he accepted the ten dollars. Nevertheless for a moment he looked at Kitty, nestling there in a stranger's arms, and he felt a delicious regret steal over him.

KILLA
T'PIG,
GEORGE

Four men in the hut. Four men hunched, their knees drawn up, all staring at the weak glimmer of the lamp. This tin, then, is a lamp, the tin with the hole in the top, and a piece of canvas tent material drooping through. It is no match for the brilliant Malayan moon flooding through the break in the nippah palm thatch.

Four men mooning, thinking about everything, for there is more in a prison than anywhere else about which to think. Yet the four rarely talk about what they think. They speak in the present, except when it is to torture themselves with memories of good food.

Tony, the one who has his hair cut short, would to some be laughable to look at, so large are his eyes, so narrow his head. But the three have become used to closely-cropped heads, and two of them remember Tony when his hair was black and shiny, curly. In those days his face had been smooth-skinned without being drawn tightly over bony contours. They do not laugh at Tony.

"Remember Luigi's?" says Tony, and the two remember Luigi's because they nod.

"A strange name for a Greek," says George. George having spent most of his time with cattle knows few Greek names, and Luigi is not amongst them.

"Omelettes," says Tony. "He could make omelettes."

"He could make omelettes," says Harry.

Harry is bigger than Tony, but his bones are as apparent, or more so, for Harry is longer in the bones. His skinny arms weave about his hunched knees. Harry used to hold a tommy-gun in those big hands so that it seemed little more than a pistol.

Only Ben Ib Id, who knew not Luigi, is smooth-fleshed, almost chunky; small however, and seeming ready to pounce.

"Your Luigi," he asks, "did he make good pork?"

There is no need to start at the mention of pork, for it is hidden away with all the other dreams for the days to come, if ever they will come; if ever, even, they could come. Hunger is never real in the final experience. It is pain, and pain is pain. The thought of hunger is the more fearsome.

George says suddenly, "What do you know about pork, Ben Hibberd?" and Ben Ib Id chuckles as though the secret is his own forever; but, of course, he will later tell it.

"Pork with curry, with pepper, with chillies," he says shrilly, mingling his words with his ridiculous laughter.

They watch the lamp, and Ben Ib Id nearly bursts with pride for his friendship with these three men, these Australians. Let the others know — his people back in Java — and they will not believe him. Friends with the tuans!

"I told them about pork," Ben Ib Id will say. "About how to cook it with curry and the chillies. (I had a little of the salt, not much salt there, you know)." Ben Ib Id has three chillies in the ragged pocket of his worn green tunic.

Tony, Harry, and the other large solemn fellow, George, are staring at the lamp, the little light that the moon almost kills. They are too solemn.

George says, surprisingly, "When we were at Kranji — when the fighting was on, that is — I killed a chook; and ate both its legs. You cooked it, Harry, remember, and you had the breast, eh?"

Harry remembers. The legs were thickly plump and white even when cooked, although the breast had browned crisply, so much so that it was a trifle leathery, like cooked newspaper. George remembers the actual mouthfuls he bit and chewed.

Well, if the moon should withdraw into itself, inverting and narrowing so that it becomes only a point of light, not affecting them, yet would they still sit and stare at the lamplight.

Food, George thinks, can kill a man's spirit if he is not careful. Can make it, too, if he is careful. It is not wrong to want food, to think about it, even. It is only wrong when you wish to have another man's food, or wish you were man enough, or devil enough, to take it. All this talk about Luigi's! Luigi, so calm, so smiling, daintily dispatching the eggs from the hot iron to the plates, and then the plates to the tables. And then, thinks George, what about everyone dispatching them to their mouths, their bellies? Down the hatch.

He looks at Harry's hands, rough, calloused with pellagra, and Harry's eyes, tired, yet sane. Harry had eaten quietly and gently at Luigi's, and had been as thoughtful as he now is, only not so weary.

"Pork," says Ben Ib Id, "I saw it today. Many porks in fact."

"Ah!" The three faces turn now, the eyes peer at him. Little Ben Ib Id, his knees tucked under him, his arms clasped about his chest, holding in the joy which is all his own, but about to be imparted.

"Ben Hibberd," says Harry. "What do you mean, eh?"

"Three porks," says Ben Ib Id. Oh, he is happy. He is telling them about the little porks he saw today. He has seen porks before, scampering about the brown legs of his children, but he scarcely noticed them then, although, now, when he thinks about it . . . yes. Perhaps these men think about their little children. Big George is still ever so solemn.

"You and your porks," George says. "What do you mean?"

Pride, pride swells, and Ben Ib Id clutches himself more. "I saw the porks down near the vegetable garden. The big pork and the little ones. They sucked her. They grow fat that way." His hands drawing apart to show how fat they grow.

"The piggery!" exclaims Tony. "By God, yes!"

George thinks about the piggery, and then says "Takahashi."

Takahashi! They see him. For ever, they think now, his face will be with them. Then what is for ever? Takahashi, little man, squat man, strange man with broad face, with gentle lips, with a terrible smile in his eyes. The yellow runt. The strange, silent guard who smiles instead of snarling.

"Yes," says Tony, "Takahashi'd know."

Takahashi knows everything. He looks as though he knows nothing. Four men afraid of Takahashi. Three fighters. Ben Ib Id afraid also. His joy dies from his eyes. He unclasps himself, but looks at George.

"You killa t'pig, Chorge?" he says plaintively.

"Porks! Pigs! I saw the pigs," says Harry suddenly. "By hell I did. I saw the little beggars. They were nudging the tapioca that grows over near the piggery. I saw one of their snouts, their little pink snouts. They'd make a great feed, only you'd never get one."

Takahashi would know. Takahashi mightn't know.

"If you could get some tapioca," says George to Harry, "and you could get some sweetbucks, Tony, and if Ben Hibberd could do the cooking . . ."

"Do the cooking," gulps Ben Ib Id, gladly. "I have curry and pepper," he announces shrilly. He pulls chillies from his pocket, three chillies, long and red. "I shall make a fine meal."

George suddenly discovers he has a store of spirit. Why do they sit crouched around this little lamp? Why are they hunched and sad and hungry and why do they think, perpetually think? The pigs that nudged. He can see their pink noses, as easily as if he were Harry watching wonderingly. Twinkle, twinkle, little nose.

"Tomorrow night?" says Tony.

"Tonight," says George. He knows that all tomorrow they will be working in the hill, and thinking. They will rest on their chunkels and look down at the vegetable patch. They will be wondering if and when it will come off. Sick with excitement they will become, and then Tony may work himself into another malarial fit, which he can so easily do.

"You get the vegetables, you two," he says, "and I'll get the pig."

"You killa t'pig, Chorge," says Ben Ib Id excitedly. He clasps himself in joy and fear. He worships George and all his quiet ways.

When the others go he cannot stay still, long, in the hut. He moves around, hunched, crouched, holding his belly, fearfully evading the brilliant patch of moonlight. He keeps fingering his chillies, looking down at them, lifting them to his eyes, looking at them nervously. His thoughts of the brown children are forgotten. He bites his nails, clutches and releases himself, and moves and fumbles with the chillies.

Tony and Harry go together, heading for the vegetable patch, and it is like crawling through the night again, with the enemy ahead. It is like blotting out a misty suffering, clothing lean shanks and bony arms with good flesh, and the spirit with eagerness. The enemy is anywhere this time. Takahashi is the enemy, on guard.

As they crawl there is no clattering of guns, no brittle noise of firing, no fearful excitement. Only the quick measured tread upon the guard's catwalk. No rifle in the hands, no bayonet. No defence at all. The guard shouts in the distance, but that does not matter, it is in the distance.

There are no pigs by the tapioca, George sees. The piggery is a stilted row of pickets, washed in moonlight, and inside the pickets sleep the big pig and the little ''porks''. The old sow is whining, her breath in long uneasy drawls. The moonlight is oily over the little pigs and the large black sow. Funny, little Ben Hibberd saying, 'Killa t'pig, Chorge''. Frightened little Ben Hibberd. The business of food.

Tony and Harry in the vegetable patch almost freeze with horror, and they are weaker than their unsteady limbs. The little pig screams and screams. His screams must be heard everywhere. George swears and throws the thing blindly, hitting it against the fence.

He had meant to catch it by its hard little mouth, hold in its alarm, bash it on the head, again and again, if need be, with the large goolie in his hand. Now he hits it hard against the fence, swinging it angrily until it stops squealing, ceases jerking, and lies still.

George stands still, expecting them to come at any moment, and there is no fear, for that has died. He feels calm, and can almost hear the bells again, as he heard them many a Sunday

19

evening, calm about their own business in a half-empty city. No bells, however, and no Nips running, no shouts and no angry cries.

He walks, trembling a bit, toward the hut. He crosses the double fence of barbed wire, and he does not know that behind him Harry and Tony are as filled with terror as he when the pig screamed.

"You killa t'pig, Chorge!" Ben Ib Id is small and afraid, is wide-eyed in incredulity. Awed he embraces himself, but not with joy. "You killa t'pig!" He almost whispers that.

"You killed it, then," says Tony. He stands at the door of the hut, and holds his stomach, as though in pain. Perhaps the tapioca, more than the fear, is a terrible burden. Food for everyone — a limp pig, and sweetbucks in Harry's shirt.

Ben Ib Id hastens. He lights a small fire, making sure the twigs blaze and have no smoke, and that the blaze is guarded by a tin surround, and then he hurries the water to the boil, and plunges the pig in the largest of his many pots. With his knife he scrapes and scrapes, taking off the hair, making the body smooth and white, clean and smooth.

George and Tony and Harry watch him, breathing heavily because they can only believe this is a dream. They have forgotten, almost, what meat tastes like. Yet there is the truth with them that the guards may have heard. They cannot believe Takahashi did not hear. They know he heard, but they cock a finger at fate and Takahashi. They watch Ben Ib Id slit the belly and draw out the guts, laying the blue mess tenderly aside.

He puts the pig, whole, into his concoction of water and condiments. Each spoonful of curry is lovingly measured, served into the belly of the pot. He crouches and stirs. It seems he is stirring for ever, before the smell comes, and the smell makes them start, almost, and they stare at Ben Ib Id, and at the pig gently boiling, humping in the pot so that its white back often shows.

George begins to forget about the pig screaming, and himself standing there, waiting for Takahashi or one of the little runts to come.

Ben Ib Id seems to have forgotten them all. He peels potatoes slowly and thoughtfully, dropping pieces into the pot as though just at their appointed time and not a second out. He stirs and droops, droops and stirs.

The smell must be all over the camp. And what if the others do smell it? They will think the Nips are having a spree. The little yellow fellows can have pigs, the men will think, and that will be all to it. They, for their part, will try to sleep through the terrible smell. Remembering places like Luigi's, they will try to fall asleep. Others will wonder when it is all going to end.

They hear Takahashi's footsteps come right up to the door. The moon dulls, about that moment, and the silver on the floor fades. Takahashi sees the fire, and Ben Ib Id over it, and the strained faces of the men who are almost sick with hunger and thought. His rifle crashes to the floor and the bayonet rattles.

He stands, smiling, in the doorway. Ben Ib Id turns and stares up at Takahashi. He remains crouching primitive and afraid. Takahashi smiles squarely and nods, and the men stand and bow, knowing it is all a farce, that Takahashi knows everything, that he heard, and has waited.

All Takahashi has to do is to turn on his heel and go marching to the Commandant's office. They will hear his tread on the hard catwalk. Then the guard will come marching down the same catwalk, and take them to Kanamoto, and Kanamoto will blaze in anger and bash them, and then put them in a closer prison, and there will be lights in the camp and shouting and everyone will turn out, and officers will be running here and there, whilst fear will be at large again, larger than it was before, and the sick men, helpless upon their beds, will wonder, and finally the tale will be told, distorted and enlarged, but such a tale cannot be distorted, nor, perhaps, enlarged. It is all distorted, this hunger business, this killing a little pig.

Nevertheless Takahashi keeps smiling, and he returns the bow, ever so slightly, and he goes over to the pot, and smiles as he sees the pig. He bends down, prods the white cooked flesh with his bayonet, and then draws the pig from the pot, stuck through by his bayonet, its body curved like a bow, its legs sticking outwards. The white steam wreathes about it in the firelight.

"Pig," says Takahashi, summing up the whole event. He looks straight at George. "You kill, eh?" he asks.

George stares at him a moment, then nods.

Ben Ib Id, mouths, over and over again, without articulation. "You killa t'pig, Chorge!"

Tony says, "I kill pig."

Harry says, "I kill pig."

Little Ben Ib Id, a brown bundle in his ragged uniform, says crouching away from Takahashi, fear in his small dark eyes, and sorrow too, says bravely enough, "I killa t'pig."

Takahashi continues to smile. He shakes his head a little, which might mean he is believing or disbelieving, but he looks at George and smiles. He caresses the pig, wonderingly, on the smooth flesh.

He chuckles a little, and then hoists the pig from the bayonet. Still chuckling he sits on the floor, and he pulls the bayonet from the boss, hacking away at the pig, gleeful, it might appear, as a child at some game.

A leg he throws to George. A leg to Harry. Another to Tony, tossed. A leg for himself. Some of the small chest for Ben Ib Id. The remainder on Takahashi's knees.

"Pig," chuckles Takahashi. He bids them eat, for they hold the pieces in their hands, wondering, not thinking of eating, not daring, perhaps.

They eat, then. Might as well eat. George eats although his gorge rises. He bites savagely at the flesh, hungry as he is, sick as he is. Tony, watching the little Nipponese, bites savagely at his. Ben Ib Id rocks a little, and weeps, almost, because he cannot understand.

George is the only one who thinks a great deal. About hunger, perhaps, about food, about what it is, and what food will do to you, and all the queer happenings of the night, and the unreality. Real enough, though, you might say, with that hound eating there. The others think that it is always like this, always for the worst. Perhaps. Perhaps.

Takahashi makes the best of a bad job, cutting it up as though he knows the English custom of sharing. He wipes his lips and smacks them, eats and grins, and looks at George and Harry and Tony, and even has a strange glance for the small Javanese. George is sure he will vomit. The pig is not pork, is not sweet, is not biting on the palate for all Ben Hibberd's curry. It is all as dead as his dull mind.

Takahashi seems to have finished, except that there is a great licking of his fingers, a matter of smiling, and then he stands. He keeps smiling at them, and saying, they know not why, ''pig, pig''; as though they understand. But they do not understand, and are silent, watching him fix his bayonet, hoist the rifle to his shoulder, go to the door, turn again, chuckling, and then disappear.

None stirs. They forget the stew in the pot, the potatoes and the tapioca and the bones they might suck. The fire might die and the stew become cold. The moon might blaze again, flooding the floor, and Takahashi go walking up the catwalk, to the Commandant's office.

The queer feeling of expectation. The smile of the smiling Takahashi. The men silent as they were before they thought about the pig or killed it. Ben Ib Id rocking himself in fear although a little time before he had been brave.

No one says he wonders what the little bastard will do, for he thinks he knows, and none has ever trusted Takahashi, never will trust him. Small hopeful thoughts grow, as ever they grow, once their minds are freed a little of paralysis.

George's mind has a terrible anger in it. He would like to smash the smiling Takahashi, smash him, yes, but he may not. He will never forgive the grinning barbarian. He will never forget his humiliation, or even the way in which he stood, himself, killing the pig, and being afraid for a moment of running, gesticulating Nips.

They hear Takahashi's footsteps upon the hard walk, but not on the way to the Commandant's office. Perhaps, then, to get the guard and take them; to procure the guard on duty. Perhaps not, too. George does not care.

He is exultant, angrily happy. He might want something to happen, the way he stands there, as though that something might whip the sullen deadly quietness which is his. Well, it is happening, it is happening.

23

Takahashi going along the catwalk, but not coming back, leaving them with their thoughts.

CHHI

Actually his name was Bobby Bree, and I don't know how he came to be called ''Chhi''. It happened somewhere back in his days when he was in the Militia, or, as we used to call them contemptuously, ''The Chockos'', meaning of course, ''the chocolate soldiers''. Not very complimentary I'm afraid, but then we were volunteers and had little time for those who practised being soldiers and for the most part did not join the Army in time of war. Time of war was, of course, time of need. However I'm not sure we had our facts correctly. I think most ''chockos'' became members of the forces. It all sounds strange of course in these days when war is outmoded, and it is very wrong to fight in an army, and so on.

To get back to young Bobby Bree. He was short, and he was stubby. He had merry brown eyes and a stubborn, rebellious chin which would flick out at a word. Tell him to do something and out came that chin. Apart from that he was a gracious sort of person, or, as we used to say, a regular guy. He would work like a Trojan, in fact work himself to weariness and then become quiet, stubborn, and a bit sullen. He would retreat into himself. When he wasn't working like that he was pleasant enough, in fact full of fun, and sometimes full of mischief. I guess everybody liked Bobby.

No one called him Bobby. They just called him ''Chhi''. He liked that. I often wondered why. Even now I wonder whether it was short for Chinese, and that was why he liked it. He had eyes which were slightly almond-shaped, slightly slanted. Yet I know for a fact that he was not Chinese. I had met his parents and his sister, and you saw no trace of Chinese in them. They were fine-looking people, especially his sister, and you could only call them Australian. Why then did Chhi like the fact of looking a bit Chinese? That is quite a question.

I have often wondered how different things might have been had our unit not gone to Malaya. Chhi might have had a different view altogether. He just might have accepted his Australian background, and settled down into it. For example, if he had been in the Western Desert there would have been none of that Chinese thing at all. There just weren't Chinese in the Western Desert.

Mind you, I'm not blaming Chhi one tiny bit. We all thought the Chinese to be fine people. As European-type persons we always seemed so large, even coarse, against their fine-boned and delicately-statured bodies. Their colour was so delicate, so even, so gracious against our variety of whites, puce-pinks, and freckled reds. They were just so different, and not only in physical appearance. They were gentle, quietly intelligent, and efficient. I guess it was their millenniums of ancient culture that awed people like me, and fiercely attracted people like Chhi. From the very beginning he was drawn to them as fine steel to an irresistible magnet.

Even a Chinese might say I had idealised his race, because not all Chinese fit the description I have just given. Take the nights we played Mahjongg with them. They would shout, even scream. Their high-pitched voices would jabber away in high acceleration, and you would think a fight was about to break out. There you would be wrong. I never saw a fight happen on that score, indeed on any score. Except, of course later when some of them emerged as Communists, but then that was much later, and the circumstances were different. They looked different, too, with their long hair streaming over their shoulders, and a certain wildness to their eyes. As I say, the circumstances were so different.

The days I am talking about are the idyllic ones at Port Dickson. Along those unbelievable tropical beaches with their clear sands and green waters and lazy palms you could have been in a picture of a tourist dream. Those Chinese homes of the rich were set back slightly from the beaches, and they were not your general, run-of-the-mill kampong Chinese houses either. They were beautifully built, dreamily architectured, and very gracious. To sit out near the beach, or on the beach, and to chat with them, the Chinese of the upper-crust — that was an experience any soldier might have coveted.

And Chhi coveted that, fiercely. He knew a few families, and one in particular. I can't remember names after all these years. I simply know the family name was Yeong. That's all I know, but I can remember the pretty, delicately-chiselled youngest daughter who really loved Chhi, and to whom Chhi, for his part, returned that love. I wasn't often invited, probably because I was gauche and shy, and anyway because I used to dream most of the time I sat with them. Probably they thought I was taciturn and impassive. To tell the truth, I didn't know how to cope with social situations. For that matter I have always had trouble on that score. I only mention my taciturn nature because I happened to go everywhere that Chhi went, but I was unable to be as sinophilic as him. I admired these people, but then I never had the passion for them which was part of Chhi's make-up.

I wish now I had paid more attention to what was happening. You probably know that the Chinese are very family-minded people. So much so that they really have very large clans, and they are very particular as to arrangements for marriages. It must all relate to the family, and so on. Our haphazard Western way of a mixed society does not appeal to them at all. I guess that is why they were very happy to have social intercourse with us, but would not have dreamed of admitting a Western soldier to their family. I never dreamed that Chhi would greatly covet being part of their family. I suppose I thought this tropical dream in which we were living would soon be over, either by recall to Australia at the best, or at the worst by some terrible act of war. That was all the thought I gave to it.

Circumstances broke our links with the Chinese families at Port Dickson. We were whisked away to Mersing on the south-east coast. All of us were put to work on setting up an intricate system of communications. The infantry dug in, making something like an impregnable fortress of that part of the Peninsula. Chhi worked with us on the lines, and we were too busy to have much social life in the district. We had a sense that war was close, and we would soon be involved in battle. The make-believe battle exercises had a touch of reality about them. The most we did was to wander in the market-place at night, drinking the cooling ices, and sampling the sweet bananas. Others simply stayed back in their camps, whiling the hours away in the canteens until the ''lights out'' bugle. The humidity was, to say the least, enervating.

Even there Chhi linked up with the Chinese family he had known at Port Dickson. As I said, the clans are large and some of the clan lived at Mersing, and some out at Endau, some twenty-six miles away. Chhi busied himself with them, but I opted out. That was a time in which I extended my writing. Some of it was dreamy poetry, but most of it was short stories. I think I had accepted Chhi's Chinese preoccupation as part of his way of life, and I left it at that.

Chhi, Col, Curly and I were in the jungle, laying line. It was midnight when we pricked our own lines to test them back to Headquarters. It was a weird experience as we heard an officer from Division Headquarters passing through the message of war. Even before Pearl Harbour intelligence had discovered a vast convoy of ships proceeding south, heading for Thailand and the Malaysian Peninsula. I watched all the faces under our flare-lamp, as I passed on the news. Col and Curly showed a certain delight, a delight of relief, but Chhi's eyes gleamed with excitement. In fact his face shone. ''About time,'' he breathed softly. Then his head went up, and he looked through the trees of the jungle to the stars which barely showed through. ''This is going to be some war,'' he said.

I remember those words now, very clearly, because it was certainly some war. Also it was some war for Chhi, and in a way the kind of opportunity he had looked for. I am still puzzled, not by his words, or even by the war, but by the whole matter of Chhi. Thinking over it now I see how little we really understand of one another, and how very, very little I understood of Chhi. I suppose my reasoning, at that time, was a fairly common one. It went something like this, "Most Australians live in the suburbs. Most suburbs are dull, hence most Australians are mediocre. Chhi comes from a suburb. Chhi is mediocre. What difference would war make? Yes, how would war change a man?"

I was soon to find out.

I'm not going to go through the story of the action. It has been written down in many places, and by people who have an eye to detail and event, which I do not. I have forgotten much more than I remember, but certain impressions remain. The spooky waiting for the Japanese to come. The first burst of excitement, exhilaration that the issues were about to be joined, and all that sort of thing, but then, as I said, the spooky waiting. Were Japanese infiltrating our jungle defences? Had they made their way through those vast minefields? Would they suddenly show themselves where we were? We received no immediate answers to this sort of question, but suddenly the skies were filled with Zeros and small bombers, and we had little to return in defence. We hid in the jungle, we worked mostly at night. We waited for the ground forces to arrive, and all the time we strengthened our defences.

Chhi seemed to work with enormous strength out of heightened excitement. He was everywhere, testing line, patrolling it, laying new lines which would keep us in communication, even if the main cables were cut. And so on. In some mysterious way he had more information than any of us, and time proved his information to be right. It was only later, in the P.O.W. camp that I thought it over and realised he had been in communication with the Chinese. They had their own intelligence lines.

The debacle of the north began. Troops began to move back down the Peninsula. It was a move designed to "shorten the lines of communication" and "to consolidate with an aim to advancing". These military rationalisations deceived no one. We were on the run. It was not easy to surrender the old image of invincibility. So we clung to it. At Mersing we were making ready for a tropical Tobruk. We would hold out, come what may.

Our time there was exciting, as Japanese troops infiltrated down the east coast, spreading out long tentacles, whilst on the west side they were pushing down with strong forces. We kept the lines intact, following up the bombings and repairing the lines. We would have to duck into the jungle as the fighter-bombers zeroed in on us. Again, I won't describe the long days and endless nights. Unshaven, rarely sleeping, constantly watching the lines, we staved off weariness in the relentless demands of the moments. Nerves frayed, irritation set in, but behind it all was a determination to become a citadel for ever, even if the west side was forced back on to Singapore Island.

One day Chhi said, ''We have to get back to Singapore Island, or we're done.''

''You're crazy,'' we said. ''We're not going to move an inch from here. They'll never dislodge us.''

Chhi looked serious. ''Fair jonniky,'' he told us, ''we're done if we don't.''

We shook our heads. ''The old Brig won't shift an inch,'' we said.

An orderly came to our tent. ''The loot wants you,'' he said. ''We're off to Singapore.''

We were stunned. Even Chhi showed surprise. ''Might be a bit late,'' he commented.

All the way along those miles we raced, trying to beat the column coming down from the north, reaching back as it was along the west coast. We had flashes of news, sudden reports of strange events, acts of heroism, bursts of victory to be followed by reluctant withdrawals. I watched Chhi as we retreated. He seemed to have changed. His stubborn chin was set, permanently. His eyes had gone hard. His very head had a grim set to it. I never saw him sleep.

But then neither did I sleep. I don't remember changing clothes in two weeks. A thick stubble grew into a flourishing beard of ginger hair, much to my embarrassment. I felt within me the same hardness I saw in Chhi. The other members of the team hardened too. Our days of mediocre suburban living were not even a thing of memory. They were blotted out. New and strange issues had confronted us and we were trying to cope with them. Life and death had new dimensions. We had joined the ancient race to which we had belonged, but which we had forgotten in the years of the Depression, and the years of existing in small houses with plots of grass, gardens and front walls. Sport and other issues seemed like the lifeless things of another world. We just did not think about them anymore. We were working out old issues, deep down in our minds, but saying nothing with our lips.

Then we were in Singapore. We had met the first elements of the retreat from the north. We mingled with them at Johore Bahru. We jostled with them on the causeway, trying to accept the traffic control of the military police. Everyone seemed to live in a black smudge as the smoke swept in from the bombed oil wells. Life was a sooty melee as we watched civilians crowd the road to Singapore, walking down one side of the main highway, whilst another stream of refugees walked away from the city.

We began the old job, laying lines, getting communications. Long ago we had left the textbook patterns. Sometimes we would lay line to a company, even to a platoon. We worked back to Division Headquarters, or forward to Battalion Headquarters, or for that matter, anywhere. Chhi was everywhere, bright as a button, hard as a diamond, frenetic as a fever, darting, throwing out line through the cable spewer, dragging it through the long lalang grass or whipping it through the rubber plantations, jumping drains, shinning up trees. He was ubiquitous, omnipresent, a bright, feverish threat.

Then they came — the Japanese. Someone had blown part of the causeway, but I guess they never intended to use that. They just came in their droves on barges, pressing, persistent, a hostile tide across the waters, getting to the shore, slipping back under the merciless throb of the machine-guns, the mortars, the heavy artillery, and even the hand-to-hand fighting. We were just behind the first line of defences, and we slipped back, keeping communication while the spitting of the Brens died, and the screams of "Banzai!" and the rattle of crackers went on ceaselessly shattering the night air. Overhead came the endless pounding of the heavy artillery from the Johore side of the Straits.

Chhi found a riderless Norton. He sat astride it, his short legs just reaching the footrests. "I'm keeping this," he said hoarsely. "We're gonna need these things."

I had always had one of them, and now I was using it most of the time. I used it until that last mad charge when I was wounded, and I saw Chhi no more. But I did see him before that charge, and what he did was most curious, although I guess now that I understand it.

He said to me, as we rode back to Brigade H.Q., "Corp, this is nearly the end. We've had it. There's no hope of things changing."

I knew he was right, but didn't like to think of it that way.

"I hear some are leaving already," I said. "That some of them are deserting."

He nodded. "That's how it would be with some of them," he agreed. "It's the crisis that shows what a man is. A man doesn't change in a crisis. He just shows what he is."

I looked at him curiously. I had never heard him say a thoughtful word. He seemed to live life rather than talk about it.

"What are you going to do?" I asked.

"Disappear," he said.

"Where?" I asked.

He grinned. "Where they'll never see me," he said.

"You mean you're going to get one of those boats?" I asked.

He shook his head. "Not likely. I know better places to go than back to Aussie."

I didn't comprehend. "Where else, then?" I asked.

He grinned, stuck out his jaw, looked hard in the eyes, and shook his head. "Can't really say," he said. "But before I go I'll do some damage."

That he certainly did. We were being pushed back on

Reformatory Road, back towards the city itself, when he did the most incredible thing. We had just passed an Indian regiment which was listless, sullen, and completely demoralised. At the time I was scornful of them, but since I have seen their point. What were they fighting for, anyway? When we passed them we heard the stutter of guns which was peculiar to Japanese weapons. Chhi pulled his Norton to the side of the road.

"Paul," he said softly. "I'm going through."

"Going through!" I echoed. "Going through to where?"

He gave a hard grin. "Just going through," he said. "Just going through."

He leaned his machine and his body towards me. "It's been good being together," he said, "and I've always appreciated it." He held out his hand. His eyes gleamed from his grimy face. "There's still time before full light," he said. "I'm going through."

He slipped a new magazine into his tommy-gun, held it in his right hand against his stomach, slightly revved his engine, and then straightened up and moved off.

"All the best," he said above the engine, and shot off into the darkness. I sat astride my own machine, weary, but listening.

Then I heard it, first the peculiar noise of the Japanese machine-guns, and suddenly, across their noise the unmistakable stutter of Chhi's tommy-gun. I sat for some moments, trying to understand, until I noticed that the Japanese stutter, and the tommy-gun stutter had both ceased, and there was the faint but distant crackle of the Norton. Even now I could not swear to it, but if it was that, then it must have been a miracle.

I never saw Chhi again.

I said I never saw Chhi again. To be honest I don't know whether I did or not. Many years later, at the time when I went to Kranji War Memorial Cemetery, I paced around the graves, trying to find his. I went into the silent arbour where they have the names of those who died, and I found it, sure enough. It had written "Signalman R.W. Bree, missing, presumed dead." It had his army number, his unit and section. Close by were other names, those of Col and Curly and men of my section. I swallowed hard and walked away.

I say I never saw Chhi. Maybe that is not true. I heard about some friendly Chinese who helped some of our fellows in their blackmarket purchases. Some of our men used to go through the wire at night, beating the guards, and getting out to where food was obtainable. They paid high prices, in Japanese dollars, or they bartered the things we had kept. Here and there a watch, or a bit of jewellery or some rare thing which was saleable. There were reports from them of a Chinese named Chai Hong who asked low prices and gave good food. He could even get some kinds of medicine. He led some of the more adventurous to where the petrol dump was, and on occasions brought a truck to them. He himself would never steal the drums of petrol, but our men did, and they drove it to a place where another driver took over, and Chai Hong paid them well for it.

Gradually I began to get the idea that Chai Hong was Chhi Bree. It was a crazy idea, and you could be forgiven crazy ideas within a P.O.W. camp. You could imagine anything there except becoming truly free. You could dream about that, but you could never really imagine it would happen.

The time I did imagine was when I had a high fever. If it had been only malaria it mightn't have been bad, but it was diphtheria, or, more correctly, a diphtheritic ulcer. I didn't know you could get diphtheria in an ulcer, but I did. I watched its white, lecherous growth spread out like a misty stain across my thigh, until the thigh began to be eaten away. Almost daily they spooned out the horrible grey patch from the centre of the ulcer, and more and more I fell into a weary fever. In the middle of the fever I saw Chhi, alive, strong, and smiling. He was smiling at me. I just didn't understand, because Chhi was dead. If he had survived those first Jap guns there would have been more behind them.

When I came out of the fever I saw someone beside me. He had a linen bag, bulging. In it was tinned food, and towgay, and dried fish, and other things. There was medicine too, sulphur drugs, and other things which would have helped me. Weak as I was I knew there was a treasure in that bag. The man who held it was one of my section. It was Hank Swain. He looked at me with pity and then said, ''Chai sent this to you. It's all for you.''

I stared at him, and then tried to sit up, but I was too weak. ''You're mad,'' I said. ''Chhi's dead.'' He looked back at me.

''I said Chai,'' he said, ''Chai Hong.''

''Oh!'' I said weakly. ''Chai Hong.'' Then I stared at him again. ''How come he sends this to me? How come he knows me?''

He shrugged his shoulders. ''Search me,'' he said. ''How would I know?'' His eyes became blank, as though he were covering something. ''Heck!'' he said. ''If that Chinese fellow wants to help you, why do you complain?''

''Who's complaining?'' I asked. ''I'm just curious. How come he knows me, and does this?''

He shrugged his shoulders, and pushed the bag under my bed. ''Look after it,'' he advised. ''You don't often come by stuff like this.''

Come by stuff like that? Man, it was a dream. Even now I see that bag, bulging with priceless food and medicine. I could feel it under the bed, and then suddenly I was tired and slept. When I awoke I thought it must have been a dream, but the bag was under the bed.

The miracle only happened once. It would be a lie to say I became strong through the food and medicine, but I know it was that which saved my life, and of course I was grateful. The fight with the ulcer was won, and I still have a weal, a long white scar to show what happened, but we won.

Some lost. They have a fine, white headstone in Kranji Cemetery, and when I go there I think about them, and the battle they lost. It always makes me grateful to Chai Hong or Chhi or whatever his real name is.

When the end came it was dramatic. The most incredible joy welled up from somewhere. It had been hidden away there for

35

three and a half years, but suddenly it burst out. Men went almost crazy, or they just became dazed with joy. They watched the first commandoes come into the camp, and then the Supreme Commander, and later the doctors, the nurses, and the food. Ah, yes, the food! That they found difficult to eat. All sorts of changes had to take place in their minds and bodies before they could feel themselves to be free and then start to live free.

My mind kept going back to Chhi or Chai or whoever it was. Some of us set out from our camp to find the good Chinese who had helped us. We searched through grove after grove, but found nothing of any Chhi or Chai. Instead we found bright-eyed, long-haired Chinese who were Communists. Some of them were searching out other Asians who had betrayed them to the Japanese through the long occupation. They were settling accounts, and working out revenge, and naming enemies. We watched helplessly from the sidelines.

On one of these searches I wandered into a kampong. There was a beautiful young Chinese, pregnant, seated on the steps outside an attap hut. I had a weird feeling that we had met, and I racked my brain to remember. The strange thought finally came into my mind that this was the Daisy we had known at Port Dickson, that she was one of the Yeong clan. Then I knew that to be stupid. She had a child, a bright-eyed little fellow of about two years of age.

I said to her, "Do you know a Chai Hong?"

For only a fraction her eyes gleamed. Then they became stolid, impassive, uncommunicative. "No, I don't," she said in beautiful English.

On a sudden impulse I said, "Do you know a Daisy Yeong?"

Again the flash, but again the quick concealment. She shook her head. "I don't know," she said, and the quaint lilt of her voice told me she was Daisy Yeong.

Of course I could have been mistaken. It may just have been a big hunger in me to believe that Chhi was still alive, even if he had married Daisy Yeong, and this little boy was his. That is why I stared at the little fellow, and of course he could have been Bobby Bree's son. Bobby Bree had looked so Chinese.

Three days later we were leaving for the hospital ship. The excitement was so intense that the thoughts of Chhi had been driven from my mind. We were put into Army trucks, seated in the back, and our new belongings and our old cherished possessions were placed in another vehicle. We left the place in convoy.

I was scarcely seeing the country as it flicked by. In fact I was in so much of a dream that I hardly realised the convoy had slowed down. Alongside the road the native population was standing, watching us. Long ago we had called out ''Hullo Joe!'' to them, because they had called it out to us. Chhi had told me once that they were not saying ''Hullo Joe!'' but some greeting which was gracious. We were answering their greeting, and shouting, ''Hullo Joe!'' We had lived with them in their suffering for these years, and they were not letting us go without love.

Finally the convoy had stopped. Unbelievably it was near the kampong where I had asked the woman with the child whether she knew Chai Hong. Hank Swain looked surprised when our truck slowed down. ''That's where we used to get the food,'' he said. ''The blackmarket food.''

I felt a chilling stab in my body. ''Not where Chai Hong lives?'' I asked.

He nodded. ''He's gone a long time,'' he said. ''He went north with the Communists before the end.''

''What about his wife?'' I asked. He shook his head. ''Never met her,'' he said.

I looked eagerly to see whether she was in the crowd, but I couldn't see her. Then I saw her, drifting out of the compound, moving towards the road. With her came a short, strong-looking Chinese, with a jutting chin, and long black hair flowing down to his shoulders.

I fought my way out of the truck, and jumped, falling on the road, then standing up I ran into the kampong. ''Chhi!'' I cried, ''Chhi, you old son-of-a-gun!'' I ran at the little man.

I saw him hesitate. Then he shook his head. ''No understand,'' he said.

''But you do,'' I said. ''You're Chhi.'' I pronounced the

37

aspirates. "You're Bobby."

He shook his head. "My name Chai Hong," he said.

I wanted to cry out, weep, sob. The driver of our truck blew his horn. Then the other drivers began to blow their horns. Tears of frustration were gathering within me.

"Bobby," I said, "Bobby, you've got to tell me it's you. Tell me. Even if you want to stay here. Tell me. You are Chhi, aren't you?"

The eyes narrowed, and then went blank. He shook his head.

I looked back at the truck. In a few miles we would be at the wharf, and then on the ship, and on our way home. And here was Chhi. Or at least I thought so.

Tears suddenly came streaming down. "Bobby! Chhi," I said, "come clean. Give me that satisfaction at least."

It was almost as though he wavered. "If you are Chai Hong," I said desperately, "then you know me. You sent me food, and medicine."

This time there was a gleam, and a half nod. Then it was Chai Hong.

The din was pounding away now, in my ears, down in my depths. The blaring of horns, the cries of the men, the shouts of officers. Some of them were coming across the kampong.

"For God's sake," I screamed, "admit you're Chhi and let me go."

Maybe I imagined I saw the eyes soften. I saw Daisy take in her breath. I always imagine it was Daisy, but then I wasn't absolutely sure.

A military police guard had taken my arm, "Come on, mate," he said, "we've got to get you to that hospital ship. We're all waiting."

That was when my heart went cold. My eyes were still crying out but Chai Hong — or whoever he was — was not taking much notice. He smiled pleasantly and nodded to the guards. They began to take me, firmly, towards the trucks.

What happened then I will never be able to swear to. Yet I believe it did happen. I swear I saw tears in the eyes of Chai Hong, and I am sure his hands, his fists, suddenly gripped tightly. I am sure that the woman put out a staying hand to him. Most of all I am sure I heard a soft voice saying, ''Paul''. I know it's crazy, but I am sure he said it, and then I saw him look towards his wife, and they did a most un-Chinese thing. They embraced, and he held her tightly while she clung to him, and the little fellow ran up and held his father's leg.

They led me to the army truck, and I was laughing and crying at the same time, and wondering about it all. I can remember a medical orderly saying, ''He needs a sedative''.

Suddenly I was very, very tired. So tired that it seemed some enormous weight was pushing down my eyelids, and I was being forced away into another world, a world of sleep and oblivion. They said I fainted, but I knew that it wasn't just fainting. I knew an enormous relief had flooded me, and also a strong pressing pain which was not a hurtful pain, but a pain in which both sorrow and joy were mixed.

Most of all I knew that this Chhi — if it was Chhi — was the truest man I had ever met. Often I have thought over that deep impression, and because of it I have realised that to be a man, especially to be a man like Chhi, is an experience whose dimensions cannot be measured. I knew that somehow no man is mediocre, not really, essentially mediocre.

I guess that you don't blame me, then, for going to Singapore, often, and you won't wonder that when I look man after man in the eye, especially men who are Chinese, and about my age, who are short and stubby with pronounced chins and bright gleaming eyes, that I will be excused for saying in my mind, ''That could be Chhi!''

Nor will you wonder that I really view every man differently from the way I viewed them before I met Chhi, especially as he seemed to shine out in the face of Chai Hong on the day we left Singapore.

THE
MIND
OF
MATSUOKO

"Matsuoko?"

"Ya, Matsuoko!"

"Matsuoko in there?"

"Matsuoko in there!"

Another area, then, of jungle to penetrate, vines to be hacked from the ancient trails where it was easy to swear no man had set foot these twelve months. Nor any animal, either. And yet it had not been months, weeks only in fact, since the tall jungle had hidden its swarms of small yellow men. Yellow men who were no longer, now, in their swarms. Driven back, pressed upon, starved, defeated, captured. Except, of course, Matsuoko.

"This time we find Matsuoko." Small Ben, the squat Javanese, was certain of it. His brown eyes assured us merrily.

An occasional hack with a parang, cutting a vine, knocking back the thorned fronds of a palm. Then stepping over the dead rotting body of a yellow soldier. Conn's quick look at it, his suspicious glance at small Ben, and then Ben nodding his head in negative fashion. "Not Matsuoko. Not Matsuoko certainly."

Not Matsuoko; neither in the flesh rotting, nor along the thin track, nor in the trees, nor hidden waiting, nor ever to be found. Matsuoko to be devoured by the blue flame of the lanky white man who pursued him.

"This Matsuoko," I said after a time, daring to say the question that had puzzled me. "You know him, Conn?"

"Yes, I know him," Conn had said gloomily.

"M'm. But not just another follow-up?"

"You could say that."

"But Matsuoko means more than that to you."

"Matsuoko is the last of them. The biggest thing yet."

And, after Matsuoko, no more Nips. There was a pleasant thought if you liked. "Mopping up" would be over. Just Matsuoko, who had committed an atrocity.

"Eight men were killed through him." If a monotone can convey intensity, Conn's voice did.

"You know all about them, don't you, Conn?"

"Very bad!" said small Ben in Malay, but Conn seemed not to hear him.

When Conn did not answer, Ben said, with the smile gone from his face, his eyes staring at Conn speculatively, "Maybe Matsuoko dead, eh?"

"No!" said Conn. Little Ben drew back from his eyes and then laughed, not nervously, but with understanding, and with great jocular confidence, "Oh no! Matsuoko not dead. Certainly never!"

"Certainly never!" Conn bent forwards again, kicking at a fallen limb in the path, hacking at a vine, pondering his own mystery of Matsuoko. The silence of the jungle falling heavily in the late afternoon, the faint sounds in the undergrowth distinct above our soft walking. Ben chatting by our side, and the whole thing unrealistic, its intensity for me lost in the familiarity time brings to places.

Then we came to a clearing, and in the clearing were huts, a whole kampong, in fact, and children playing in the centre of the village. As we appeared they ran up the fragile steps of the huts, and a few squat Javanese appeared.

"What news?" shouted Ben happily.

"Good news," they said, returning the formality. Conn stared at them without expression.

"Matsuoko," said small Ben, his brown eyes gleaming, his face lit with joviality.

"Ah," they said. They nodded and began speaking savagely. Ben listened to them, his head cocked to one side, and Conn never blinked an eyelid.

"There," they said and pointed to the jungle. They appeared immensely relieved, as though the shadow of Matsuoko was about to depart from their lives, which, of course, it was.

"Matsuoko," they said, "*tida bagoose.*"

"Very bad," I agreed, and Ben clapped his hands and gabbled softly. Their eyes lighted with real pleasure. When Matsuoko went, that would be the last of Nippon, and the dread occupation of their jungles. The tapioca would be theirs, the corn, the yams, and the pardi. Ah, yes, the pardi.

"And the pardi?" Ben asked.

The laughter left their eyes and they stared speechlessly at the jungle, at the ground, and finally, fearfully, at Conn. His eyes were very blue now, inquiring.

"Pardi through there," they said.

Ben spoke something in Malay, but they shook their heads. They knew nothing about the pardi, only that it had happened somewhere. And the pardi was green now, soft and flowing. We could see it through the stems of the graceful fronded palms. Only beauty on the waving green. They shook their heads slowly.

Conn nodded to them. "Matsuoko," he said in a strange dry voice, staring at the field of mud and rice.

Matsuoko hidden in the last of the jungle, the beginning of the new jungle which rose towards the hills, the vastness of it spreading away. To remain in it could be only death by starvation for Matsuoko, and yet it was understandable that he should try to hide. Through the strip that led by the pardi and into the leafy thickness of the new jungle the Malays led us. Then, when we had gone some distance, treading the thickness of undergrowth on a scarcely-used track, they stopped, and before us was Matsuoko.

Strangely enough it was not at Matsuoko I looked, but Conn. I expected hate and triumph, but there was neither of these. His eyes did soften a trifle, and his lips did relax, but it seemed more relief than anything. Then he said, almost goodhumouredly, "Ah, Matsuoko!"

He was seated on a bamboo platform, his legs crossed, yogi fashion, his skinny arms resting in his lap. He wore a loincloth of sorts, but it was covered with his own filth. His skin was dried and yellowed, like aged parchment. His eyes were huge in their sockets and hot as they stared. His face was black around the mouth and chin with a growth of thick dark hair, longer even than the hair of his head which had been not long since shaven. He was a haggard animal, worn out by dysentery, and drooped there on what might almost have been his death bier. The covering above him had rotted and left him exposed to what sun filtered through the gloomy jungle.

It was queer seeing this Matsuoko there.

"Five days without food," one of the men muttered to small Ben. "When it finished, no more food." He thrust out his hands angrily, deprecating the necessity for explanation. Ben nodded assuringly, and the group fell silent.

"Ah," said Conn again, almost tenderly this time. "Matsuoko."

It was impossible for Matsuoko to read any meaning into those words. I could not read them, but Matsuoko, still and watching, would not take his eyes from Conn's face. Dry petrification in that cruel flesh, perhaps, but in the eyes, knowledge. The remainder of us did not exist.

Then he said in a dry harsh voice, "Kanamoto, me."

The natives looked surprised, almost offended. One of them said indignantly, "Matsuoko!"

The Nipponese on the platform shook his head with strange dignity. "Kanamoto," he insisted.

"Kanamoto," said Conn slowly. He passed his tongue across thin dry lips and shook his head, not without belief, but with faint incredulity. "Kanamoto?" he repeated wonderingly. Then he smiled gently.

The sick soldier seemed to gain assurance from that. He straightened perceptibly, as though gathering his dignity fully about him. In a way I was forced to admire him.

"Ha!" said Conn suddenly. He stepped forward and took between the thumb and forefingers of his right hand a hair of Matsuoko's face. I thought he was going to pull it. I had seen that happen often, though not with Conn. Conn retained it, looking into Matsuoko's eyes, but he did not tug. "Kanamoto, eh?" he said quietly, without the trace of a sneer. "Matsuoko, I think," he said.

When the soldier made no response he said suddenly, in the

same harsh voice the sick man had used, but in Japanese, something which made the sick man start. He looked fully at Conn and shook his head. Conn let his hand drop slowly. Then he said to the kampong natives, ''Carry this man.''

They seemed reluctant to do so, staring at Matsuoko with hate and some fear. Nevertheless they wrested some poles from the platform, some nippah-palm and improvised a stretcher. At the kampong they made the stretcher more secure and we followed it in silence, Conn staring down at the prisoner, but not speaking. When we reached the camp Conn took him to the hospital instead of a prison cell.

''I can't understand you, Conn,'' I said.

He looked at me a moment, frowned and said, ''Matsuoko's a sick man.'' He smiled, becoming a soldier again. ''Or Kanamoto, as he liked to be called,'' he said mockingly.

It took three weeks to save Kanamoto from dysentery and debility, and make certain he would live. Then two weeks to strengthen him, and another month to fatten him to normal strength. He had been a sick man for a long time, and yet the power of his personality had forced those kampong Javanese to take him food when they hated him.

I could easily visualise the sick Kanamoto seated upon his platform, seeing the Nipponese planes disappearing from the sky, the sounds of war fading with him brooding over a pardi-field and eight men bowing to him and the glory of Nippon, bowing until their noses touched the cold mud. Bowing even deeper. And Kanamoto watching, whilst he remembered, hoping the leaves would part and white rice be thrust before him, with perhaps a mess of tapioca, a tasty slice of white pork or the rich salty tang of dried fish. But no food, no human being, no soul to hear him groan and writhe as the disease bit deeper.

In the early days of his treatment Kanamoto was silent, and even grateful for the treatment he received. Then he became arrogant, contemptuous of soft usage. Conn, who had nearly wept at Kanamoto's lapse into unconsciousness, now stared at

him thoughtfully and even more thoughtfully when he transferred the patient to the prison cells.

Conn's treatment of Matsuoko puzzled me. On the one hand
I could conceive of him trying to save the Nipponese in order to
have him tried and hanged, but because I knew Conn better
than others I was sure there was more to Conn's care of the
prisoner than that. He had even dressed Kanamoto in
Nipponese soldier dress and given him a sergeant's rank, so that
Kanamoto could fairly claim to have been rehabilitated in mind
as well as body. It was apparent to me that Conn saw something
special in Kanamoto.

Nevertheless I was surprised when Conn sought me out one
night and began discussing the matter.

"This Matsuoko," he said. "You know, there is no way of
proving he is Matsuoko."

"You have photographs," I said.

"Oh, I know he's Matsuoko," he said, "but it has to be
proved. Most of them don't keep up the pretence long. Usually
they admit it, as you know, and are proud to do so, especially if
they know they are bound to die."

"And Matsuoko'll do the same, eh?" I said.

Conn sat staring for some time. Then he said, slowly, "Oh,
no, he won't." He looked at me with eyes surprisingly gentle.
"I think his crime was too personal to admit."

I knew Conn had some private knowledge of the working of
the Jap mind, so I did not contradict him. His statement on the
surface was incredulous. "Yet," I said, "any Nip would have
done it."

"Oh, yes," he admitted easily, "any Nip *would* have done
it. To execute eight airmen would have been an intense delight
— for the glory of Nippon."

"Then you'll get him," I said triumphantly. "He'll be glad
to admit it, later."

My enthusiasm scarcely touched him. "Yes, I will get
him," he said, "but not in that way. Matsuoko won't admit it
that way. He killed the airmen for Matsuoko, that's what he
did."

I shook my head. It was difficult to follow Conn.

45

"Say," Conn said, "we failed to prove he was Matsuoko. Then he would be just any prisoner. He would go free. If he went free then he would be free to kill himself if ever he wished, and so be happy. Or, on the other hand, being the queer individual he is — and he is an individual — then he might prefer to keep his life and his memories." Conn stared at me and said in a dry voice, "He is not one of Nippon's honourable ones, you know."

"Well," I said, "I've seen Nips made to confess before today."

He stared at me.

"One man," I said, "pulled out a beard, hair by hair. Mind you, Conn, he had a brother in a Jap camp, and he felt badly. Another time he whipped the calves from a Jap's legs. Tanaka was that Nip's name."

"Yes," said Conn. "I know. But that isn't right."

Conn saw I was amazed. "He was only doing what he feared himself," he said. "Just equalling the crime," he said, "so that in the long run the Nip really won."

I could not understand that, and Conn knew it. At other times I suppose he might not have cared, but because he was in an unusual mood, excited I think, he began arguing the matter. "You'd hate a big skunk of a Nip to stand over you when you were helpless," he said, "and you'd only see him as cruel and merciless. Yet you would do the same now and feel justified.

"Now, I'll tell you something," he said suddenly, and his eyes had lost their ice. "I've never told this to anyone, Tony. We won't be together for long now and when we part we might never meet, and even if we do I'll be in different clothes and you'll think then that I am different." He paused and said in a tone of exultation, "I will be different, too."

He began a sort of story. "I was an insurance clerk before I enlisted. I suppose that surprises you. Well, it surprises me, too. When I enlisted I suppose I came to life, if you could call it that, for the first time. War then was going to be glory for me, like it is to you and some of the others. I was going to go over the top. I was sure for the very first time that I was really alive.

"There were others with me, too, those who had escaped

their wives, families, the monotony and the work of life. They were just as keen. They came to life, I suppose you could say. You could talk to them, over a drink, at nights on bivouac. I suppose they talked as they hadn't done before.

''When final leave was over I was glad, but looking back on it sometimes, Tony, I think it is as unreal as my old clerking days. The ship that took us to Singapore, the moon on the ocean at night, the guns sticking up above the top-deck, beer everywhere, men talking, and at heart anticipating. Then Singapore Island, green like these islands here, and natives clamouring for our pennies. Then the train taking us north.

''We moved off in the night and went across the Straits of Johore. I thought that night was the very best in my life. It was like dreaming properly for the first time and even having that dream come true. The lights on the waters of the Straits, the smell of it; the smell of the East; and on the northern shore of the Straits the buildings and palaces in the late evening, lit with stars it seemed. Then the jungle.

''I sat in the last carriage and stared at it, and thought all life was very wonderful, very mysterious. But it was all imagination. It's wrong, though, Tony, for a man to lose his sense of mystery and beauty, and have to put it down to imagination. Strangely enough it was the most real thing that ever happened to me. I could see a whole world of beauty reaching down to the South, and it was for us to defend. Even when we trained, or went on leave, or hit the high spots, it was still the best thing I had known, the very best thing.''

Conn Webster, as he spoke, had become human. Now his head was resting in his clasped hands as he stared at the ground. His lips had resumed their normal decent fullness, and his eyes were warm and living. I wondered, almost wistfully, about the strange days of that ghost force up on the Peninsula, and yet it was difficult to envy them. Nevertheless, they had had an experience which could never be ours. Most of all I wondered about Conn Webster, and why he should be sitting there, talking to me about his hidden past.

''We thought then that they'd leave it until after the monsoons, but they didn't, of course. Long before they landed, long before they reached us I had begun to wonder about fighting. Most took it for granted, as most still do, and some seemed scared when you caught them unawares with a question, but I never knew properly what my feelings were. At the back of my mind I wondered if I was all I had believed myself to be.''

Conn had been talking to me, but more, I think, to himself. Now he looked at me and said, ''You know what it is to be scared of being scared, don't you, Tony?''

''Yes, I do,'' I said. ''Most of us do.''

He nodded. ''Well, I was. When the balloon went up we were on our battle-stations. Different, see, from going on the offensive. Waiting all the time. I began to think I couldn't do it. I began to remember I had been an insurance clerk, that I was, underneath, still an insurance clerk, one at heart and not the great Conn Webster, that born fighter. Looking at the others, the confident ones, I began to think they were the really born fighters, and that I was outside them.

''I managed to fight these thoughts at times, and then when the Nips did land it seemed all so easy. We actually ambushed them in places and wiped them off with artillery barrages and laughed at their silly waving of flags, their cries and their shouts and their crackers. I knew then that I wasn't scared. Then there wasn't much fighting in our area, as the other coast had been broken in its lines and we were forced to retreat to the island from the mainland.

''It was a week before they landed on the island, but that week worked on me. We were cooped up in a small area, bombed and gunned and shelled continuously without much ack-ack defence and with no air defence at all. That part didn't matter, though. It was the fighting I was thinking about. Then they landed.''

''The magic had gone out of the Straits then, Tony. The whole romantic dream was drivel. But I still believed I was a soldier and I wanted to be that more than anything, as though it was what counted, and it was, too.''

Conn was talking to himself really, although he fancied I was the only listener.

"When they landed it was terrible. I was down on the beach on a Bren. We kept at it until our magazines gave out. Then a runner brought us more, and we started again. After a time our Number Two was killed. We kept firing until they were so thick we had to go. We raced back into grass and scrub, carrying the gun, firing here and there. After a while there were only two of us left, and I wasn't firing. Harry — that was his name — he kept working, and I was feeding the magazines. All in a blaze of glory, too. Until they were nearly on us.

"You could see them coming, all right. They didn't care. There were too many for them to care. They threw their crackers into the air, and fired tracers, and laughed and joked like the devil on a holiday and screamed and shouted and cheered, and whirred rattles and flung bungers. You'd call it funny now, but it wasn't then. Think of it, Tony, the first to face that sort of thing, something which we know now, but didn't know then.

"We kept firing until Harry was killed. Somehow nothing seemed to hit me. It was my big chance. There was still some ammo but I didn't wait. I left everything and ran. Can you see what I did?"

"Anyone would have, Conn," I said.

He shook his head, but when he spoke he was arguing with himself, going over an old discussion, assessing facts, summing up, condemning.

"No, a born soldier may be careful, but he doesn't care in those moments," he said. "I did. When I got away from them I ran like a little kid and I cried like one until I was well out of danger." Conn stopped and looked up at me. "You know," he said slowly, "I had the feeling those Nips were laughing at me, that they knew what I was."

I remembered Conn's cold stare at Matsuoko, and Matsuoko's unwavering stare in return.

"You might think that silly, but it stuck in my mind. I wandered through the scrub and stuff until I met up with others. Things weren't going to schedule, but we settled down and waited for them to come through. It was early morning and they didn't. Then, when the sun came up we withdrew quietly to what they were always calling 'appointed positions'.

"We did that for days, losing ground all the time, being shelled and bombed and machine-gunned out of positions, being pushed back inch by inch, and I was never wounded. That was the strange thing about it, Tony: never wounded. You'd have thought I'd have been glad about that, and that I would have risked more than I did. But I wasn't glad. I kept thinking all the time that it was useless, anyway, and that I'd escaped so far, and I'd make sure I escaped altogether.

"Escaped altogether!" Conn echoed those words, almost as a question. His eyes dulled, his face relaxed. "It's hard to tell this part, Tony. We got pushed back properly and the battalion broke up. We re-formed into another battalion back at base and went forward again, but we were a different crowd. There were reinforcements who panicked at the slightest thing. You never knew where you were, but I suppose you'd say I was lucky. I was with the best of our old company, in the one section. We moved forward in the late afternoon, the sort of afternoon you spend at home playing tennis or chatting over afternoon-teas, or taking your girl on picnics. It was cool and had a soft light about it. Then, when darkness fell, we went forward. This time we had to attack and break through. It was madness, of course, and I knew it, and I think most of us knew it, but what I knew, more than any of them, was that the end must come sooner or later and why not in the very best way?"

Conn stopped again and stared at me, his eyes no longer dull, but filled with accusation. "Why not the best way, Tony? To charge and be damned! That's what the others thought, and when the guns began, the artillery and the machine-guns and the mortars, they didn't care for officers, anyone or anything. They charged, all of their own accord. They'd been told it would come to that, and it had. I was in the section, but I didn't go forward. I told myself I was waiting for orders. Waiting for orders, Tony. And then some of us fled, and I was with them. When we were past the supporting troops we were able to sit down and rest for a time, but I didn't wait to rest. I went on into Singapore itself, where there wasn't any fighting at that time. I just walked into Singapore.

"It's funny, I suppose, but I remember getting coffee at a hotel. There were plenty of soldiers there, and some kid — a newly-arrived reinforcement, probably — spilled it over himself because his hand was shaking. Then he began to blubber. The old lady who was serving the coffee came across and put her arm around him. She smiled at him and said something. The kid had got up by this time. I could see he was going back. When she looked at me the smile went off her face and out of her eyes. She just went back to her coffee."

Conn laughed. "I suppose the kid went back and was killed. I never went back. I waited in Singapore for another day, and then I got on to a boat that was taking civilians. I was dead by that time. I had ceased thinking, or I only had one thought, to get away."

"I never knew about this," I said.

Suddenly Conn seemed different, as though his life with us had been a weird pretence.

"So I suppose I did die," he said, walking away, staring into the camp compound. "Anyway, I was dead on that ship. I lay on the decks night and day until we reached Java. I was just alive enough to see it all, time and again, what I had run away from, from that moment when Harry was killed. I wasn't bomb-happy, and I wasn't scared. When the seas were rough, or the bombers came after us it didn't matter. When we were taken off at Java and put into cells it still didn't matter. When they put us on the boat to come home I didn't care. Not until we reached the Heads at Sydney.

"It was seeing those Heads which brought me to life. I knew then that something had gone wrong, what it was almost, but I couldn't believe it. Strangely enough it was all mixed up with having been an insurance clerk in a quiet city, a soldier racing through the jungle that night, running from the shrieking Nips, coming into Sydney through the Heads. I knew there could never be another chance."

"Why couldn't there?" I said.

"Malaya had fallen," he said. "I couldn't go back there and fight it again. I couldn't even start that war again, or be one of the captured prisoners. It was ended for ever."

Conn looked almost pitiful. "You'll have to hear the rest of it," he said. "They didn't know whether or not to put us in prison. I had some vague idea of blotting out the past, and when I volunteered to go north they let me. Others didn't want to go. I went back into infantry to begin with, and fought pretty well. No running away this time, and it seemed good to be on the offensive.

"Then I thought I'd like to get closer to them. As you know we never saw much of them in infantry, not to speak of, anyway. I wanted to know if they were braver than us, as brave as they made out, at rock-bottom, below the training of fanaticism. I started to learn the language. It didn't take long. Strange that, when you think I couldn't learn simple French at school."

Conn stared fully at me. His face was composed, but there was a slight cynical twist to the lips. "Well, that's it," he said. "That's all."

"All?" I echoed.

"Yes," he said. "Now you can see why I just can't whip a confession out of Matsuoko. He has the upper hand, morally."

"You're a queer cuss, Conn," I said. "Granted you missed the bus in Singapore, but what about what you have done since?"

"And what have I done since?" he asked, his eyes beginning to turn cold.

"Well," I protested, "you have two mentions to your credit."

He laughed. "Bravery," he said. "What's that? What's in driving yourself on, or being driven because of the thing that is nagging at you, the old fear of fear, the fear of failing again, of adding sin to sin, so that you can never live with yourself when it is all over? That isn't bravery."

"You're crazy," I said. "Of course it is. You just weren't experienced. Why, I've known cases . . ."

"So have I," Conn said. "You're a fool, Tony. I thought you'd understand, even if the others didn't. Don't you see that when Matsuoko had those men before him he had the upper hand, everything in his way. Then he told them to die, and they had to die — because Matsuoko said so.''

"Because Matsuoko said so," I repeated mechanically.

"And now Matsuoko has to die," Conn said; "but he has to die because he is not worth living with — living with himself. Matsuoko has to pay for those little Japs who made me run," Conn said slowly. "He will to prove to me that I was wrong, that they would have done it, too, that I wasn't any more pitiful than they would have been."

"And that helps?" I asked.

"Listen, Tony," Conn said. "If Matsuoko had had me in the pardi-field I wouldn't have cringed. I wouldn't have cared, or been afraid, not like I was in Singapore. I could have thought clearly as I do now, as I never did at Singapore. Matsuoko can think clearly. I've often wished to die, but I couldn't. You might say it was written that I couldn't. Matsuoko doesn't want to die, but he will, and he will want to die honourably, but he won't be able. We don't commit *hara-kiri* to escape our deserts, Tony, and Matsuoko won't either."

"Then I can't see it, Conn," I said. "It's all too complex for me."

"You'll see," he said calmly. "Just watch Matsuoko."

"Those eight airmen," I said suddenly. "Where are they buried?"

"Remember the pardi?" he asked.

I remembered it and the downcast looks of the natives.

"We don't know where," he said. "Even little Ben doesn't know that. He only had it on hearsay. But Matsuoko knows, and he knows we don't know."

"We could dig," I said.

Conn laughed, his old icy laugh. "So we could," he agreed. "But we won't. It would take a long time. No, Tony, we won't bother to dig."

I did watch Matsuoko — and Conn. Before the Nipponese was transferred to the cell, and in his last arrogant days in the hospital, I watched him and Conn. Conn always took me with him.

Once with Matsuoko he would simply stare at him, a cold meaningless stare. At first it confused Matsuoko, but later he became almost triumphant about it, not that he showed it in expression, but you knew, even felt it. It was as though he wished to unnerve Conn, but I knew he would not succeed. For myself I had a great contempt for the little sergeant. I knew, with Conn, that he was a murderer at heart, and that his atrocity was personal, a gesture of personal hatred or fear. Conn would have known best what it was.

When Matsuoko went to the prison cell he seemed no less arrogant. He expected water when he wanted it; even cigarettes, and would attempt to bully the guards. They ignored him, and he seemed to think that was a great triumph for him. Perhaps he wanted them to dance attendance, but I think not. Gradually I became interested in Matsuoko, almost as interested as Conn. Only the guards had little time for his tactics. ''Why don't you starve the fat bastard?'' they asked him.

''He'll be better for the killing,'' Conn told them; but I knew it wasn't what he meant.

After a time Matsuoko began, I think, to look forward to Conn's visit with a fascinated dread. I would have hated to have had those cold eyes upon me, neither commanding nor inquiring, eyes without purpose, you might say, yet some purpose lurking behind them. There was no personal hate in Conn. But there was nothing, either, on which Matsuoko might feed his pride as a son of Nippon, his own individual arrogance. At first he had been able to think Conn soft for saving him, and then it might have dawned upon him that it was for a killing, but he was cunning enough to know he was safe. Some second instinct must have warned him to murder the few natives who had seen the killing of the airmen, even the one who had spoken, in a prison, to little Ben.

How Conn knew that Matsuoko could speak English I do not know, but I saw the sergeant start when Conn said to me, in his cell, ''This man will be known as a coward when he goes back to Japan. He has surrendered.''

Matsuoko almost spoke, but his fingers compressed into his palms.

''But they are all like that,'' Conn went on calmly, ''when the fighting is over. They fight under hysteria.''

Matsuoko was giving Conn small darting looks.

When we left the cell I said, ''You had him there, Conn. It's the first time I've seen him roused.''

''Of course,'' Conn said.

I thought Conn should have followed it up immediately, but he had different plans. There were times when I saw the very sweat stand out on the head of the stocky Nipponese, but he never spoke. Often Conn would ask him, almost dully, ''You Kanamoto, eh?'' and always Matsuoko would give his small secretive smile and nod. ''Me Kanamoto.'' Conn would smile, too, faintly, and the Nip never seemed compensated for his small triumph.

One day he told him that Matsuoko, when he was found, would be hanged for the murder of eight airmen and many natives. Kanamoto seemed politely interested. Time and again I could have smacked his fat face, but Conn seemed not to care.

The next day Conn said to me, in English, and before Matsuoko, ''This man is afraid to admit his crimes. For the true son of Nippon it is no crime. Only to the boastful who murder. They were helpless, but he did not know Nippon would lose, otherwise he might have thought better.''

He turned and regarded Matsuoko with a cold stare.

In the cell, on the second day, Conn gave me a talk, in English, about the theories of Nippon, about honourable death, and those Japanese ethics so familiar to us. If I had not known it was for Matsuoko's benefit I would have been bored.

The third day brought the report that Matsuoko refused to eat his food. Conn went to the cell immediately, and asked Matsuoko in politest tones to eat his food. ''We wish to return an honourable fighter to his homeland,'' he said, ''and if you do not eat you will die.'' He stood for a time gazing at the sullen sergeant.

The next day Conn asked him a question. ''You will be a great hero when you return to your homeland, eh?''

Matsuoko regarded him with slow cunning. ''I do not think so,'' he said, and Conn knew it to be ambiguous deliberately.

Matsuoko ate because of the bayonet at his stomach. While he ate Conn talked to me about the Matsuoko who, when he was found, would be hanged, and who would be unable to commit himself to an honourable death. Conn shook his head and looked at Matsuoko.

I thought Matsuoko would never break, and that all Conn's efforts were doomed to be fruitless. In his own way, Matsuoko had the upper hand. We were convinced he was Matsuoko, but we had no worthwhile evidence. Nor would we have cared much. Matsuoko could easily have died, one way or another, but that Conn would not allow.

Ben was brought in. It was evident he disliked Matsuoko, but he seemed not to show it. Instead he was uproariously humorous, as indeed Conn intended him to be. Immobile, Conn would stand and regard the prisoner, and Matsuoko showed both contempt and bewilderment, although gradually the contempt died. Ben would withdraw silently and Conn would stand watching him. Conn was always careful to explain that this Ben had been a Nipponese prisoner, and that while in prison he had been told about the execution of eight airmen by one Matsuoko.

Then, suddenly, Conn seemed to have changed his tactics. He began a rapid-fire of questions to Matsuoko. Did he have a wife? Would he be glad to go back to her? Did he love the Emperor? Did he like fighting? Was he glad it was all over? Did he fear death? Did he believe in the old-time religion of Nippon? Then Conn cracked a few jokes at which he laughed himself, uproariously, as though, with Ben, he seemed to share some tremendous joke, but the sergeant regarded him without a smile, and seemed, if his eyes betrayed anything, to be even more fearful of this new development.

Ben was allowed to come in occasionally and look at Matsuoko. To nod his head smilingly and say, "This Matsuoko. Oh, yes, certainly."

Perhaps Ben was the last straw. Matsuoko began to lose his calm. He had long lost his customary arrogancy and swagger. He would not refuse meals, but ate them with pitiful relish. The guard reported him as staring through the window continuously, as though on the outlook for Conn. When he saw Conn coming he would pace his cell, although by the time we arrived he would have fairly well concealed his agitation.

I was growing excited, was as involved almost as much as Conn. It seemed something hung in the balance, and was to be decided by this experiment.

One morning Conn went up to the sergeant, nodded and said, "Good morning, Matsuoko."

Matsuoko said nothing. The next morning little Ben came, nodded towards the prisoner and said, "Him Kanamoto," after which he roared laughing. He crouched on the floor in imitation of the sick Matsuoko and said, mimicking the prisoner, "Me Kanamoto!"

Then, looking at Conn, he said, "Him good Nippon soldier."

When Ben had left the cell Conn peered through the window of the door to see where the guard was stationed. He was nowhere near the cell. Conn walked up to the sergeant, stared at him, and waited until Matsuoko positively trembled. Then he walked towards the door, but somehow his pistol became detached from the holster and clattered to the floor. Conn was extraordinarily slow to act, and Matsuoko was on to it before he turned. Then Matsuoko backed away, grasping the pistol, snarling gutturally.

Until then, I suppose, I had never fully understood the depths of Conn's experience, nor his claim to another experience which would cancel his past shame. It was as though, in those moments, I fully understood the fear which had been his, the shame following it. Long ago any of us could have whipped a confession out of the yellow prisoner, but it may have been, too, that Matsuoko would have defeated us. I don't know. We would never have got it in the way Conn did. When he faced Matsuoko he never moved.

Instead, he looked at Matsuoko, and Matsuoko at him. The contortion in the Nip's face died to smoothness. I was helpless, too, having no pistol. The guard was too far away to know what was happening. To shout would have meant death to one of us at least.

Conn continued to stare, his cold eyes on the small yellow man, and the small yellow man, pistol in hand, began to show fear. Then his hand trembled. At first I could not believe that, but when I thought over those weeks of staring, strange questionings, contempt in his eyes more so than in his words, I began to understand. I knew this Conn was not the man who had run at Singapore. He was a man of whom anyone might have been afraid, and with justification.

Conn did not speak. But Matsuoko did. ''I am Matsuoko,'' he said in perfect, though lilting, English. He smiled triumphantly at Conn. He listened for the guard's tread, and when it did not come he said, ''I have killed many.'' He smiled again, and his eyes were on Conn. I doubt if he could have shifted his gaze. ''I would shoot you,'' he said, ''but it is not honourable, seeing you have saved my life.''

Conn said nothing and Matsuoko was disappointed. ''It is true I committed some killings of airmen. It was very good. They died as all men must die. I gave them honourable death.''

His fear of Conn seemed to have died. ''Now,'' he said, ''I die honourable death.''

It was queer watching him place the pistol to his stomach — not to his head or heart, although he placed his free hand over his heart — and it seemed queerer that it should happen in a prison cell where he was a prisoner, and where, only a dozen yards away, there was a guard. Perhaps I should have shouted, but that would have been incredibly foolish, so instead I watched the incredible escape from dishonour of the fat Matsuoko, no longer diseased, but in possession of full health and his mental faculties.

''You will not die now,'' said Conn slowly. He kept Matsuoko's eyes to his. He will hypnotise him, I thought; but it was madness to think that. Such moments seem to move slowly, so much thought can be crowded into them, so much understanding, as though, throughout the business of life, nothing is irrelevant, unrelated. Let him shoot himself, Conn, I was saying. It is better for him to die that way. Then I thought that Matsuoko might want to kill us as a last fine gesture to the Nippon whom he had nearly betrayed.

But Conn had taken the courage from him. If he could wound himself, then courage would immediately return.

58

"There is no death for you, yet, Matsuoko," Conn said, and I was reminded, strangely, of the Conn Webster asleep on the ship, with his shame haunting him, and wanting to die, not knowing or caring, living and dying being the same, both terrible, yet both to be desired and hated.

I could understand now. Here was Matsuoko escaping because death was honourable. But Matsuoko would never have killed himself had not Conn awakened that shame within him. "We can't have that way out," Conn had told me. "We can't commit *hara-kiri.*" And again he had said, "He won't admit his crime. It was too personal for him to admit."

But Matsuoko had been any man then, arrogant in his power, abusing it, striking fear or courage into the hearts of dying men, yet making them die, nevertheless. It was nothing to do with war, as Conn had said. It was too personal to admit.

Then Matsuoko squeezed the trigger. His eyes were upon Conn's, fearfully, pleading almost to be allowed that escape, but when he pulled the trigger there was only a click. Rage broke in Matsuoko and all his proud arrogance was shattered. He forgot his marvellous doom, and pointed the pistol at Conn. It clicked again, and with the fury of desperation, his eyes gleaming in live rage, he threw it.

It caught Conn on the shoulder and dropped to the floor. I picked it up. Conn never moved. His eyes were on the trembling sergeant.

Cold eyes. Eyes of white-blue flame. Flame within ice. But above all eyes that knew the secret and the shame of Matsuoko.

Then Matsuoko broke. His hand gesticulated, clawed, words poured like a torrent from his lips, babbled, stuck in his throat, emerged in anger, in rage, but mainly in babbling terror, and all the time Conn stared at him, speaking not a word.

I looked down at the pistol, and marvelled at the foolish Matsuoko, the foolish Conn. There were only two empty chambers, and the pistol had been set for them. Whether deliberately or not I did not know, then or ever.

"Get a guard, Tony," Conn said. "We'll take him there while he's like this. He can dig the bodies up, with his hands if he likes. I think he would."

59

Conn had begun to glow, as though life, long withheld in the back-reaches of himself, was now beginning to flow, to warm him. It was as though a vacancy was being tenanted, and with a living being. Yet his eyes upon Matsuoko were cold, although his voice, when he spoke, was almost genial.

"He can grovel in the mud if he likes," he said. He nodded Matsuoko into temporary silence and repeated, as though in some form of symbolism. "Grovel in the mud, Matsuoko."

TO
COMMAND
THE
CATS

Denny met Morgan Todds in the railway waiting-room at Snowy Vale. "Gentlemen's Waiting-Room'', the notice said outside, and Denny thought it was the first time he had seen a notice like that.

When he entered the room it was cold, and just before midnight. There were six servicemen and ex-servicemen. Some wore their jungle greens without colour-patches, and all were shut in thick greatcoats, shivering as Denny himself, although it was not quite winter. Morgan Todds was in contrast, being a small figure, clothed in shiny black, and huddled upon a waiting-room chair. He looked at Denny when he walked in, then, with a shiver, tried to withdraw into his black, his shiny black.

Denny did not know him as Morgan Todds, ringmaster of the circus camped beside the station, and so he did not speak to him. Morgan Todds did not speak either. Some of the servicemen were talking, and one was saying how he had managed two hundred rabbits in two days; how he had a good bait and guaranteed. There was a glowing from the fires of the circus, but in the waiting-room there was no fire, until one of the men said he would "scrounge" some coals, and in a few minutes was back with live coals on a shovel, glittering and spluttering with good red heat.

Morgan Todds spoke to Denny. "You take a seat here," he said. "It's not far from the fire."

The grate was cluttered with last year's ashes, and the hot coals began to die.

"You want timber on that," said Morgan Todds. "Go

down to the circus lines there, and tell 'em Morgan Todds sent you. They'll give you some deal.'' He stared down at his hands. ''I'd go myself only for this hand,'' he said.

Denny looked at the smallish man. He had one hand bandaged, and the bandage was a little old, slightly soiled.

They brought the timber back, and put it on the coals. It crackled and exploded in the large waiting-room. The soldiers were talking about Nips, and one said he had been a prisoner under them for a day. Morgan Todds looked at the soldiers talking, and leaned across to Denny.

''It's going to be colder than this,'' he said.

Denny nodded, recognising the urge for conversation. He shifted closer to the circus man, and then looked down at the bandaged hand.

''The cats,'' said the man in black. ''You call 'em lions, but we call 'em cats, mostly.

''It's the little 'uns,'' he said, ''that are no trouble. The big 'uns that are the trouble.'' He pointed down to the circus. ''I'm ringmaster there,'' he said. ''I'm Morgan Todds. I command the cats.''

''Pretty tough cats,'' said one of the servicemen.

''Old Gouger got me,'' said Morgan Todds, ''and he's a nasty piece of work.''

Denny spoke for the first time. ''It must take guts,'' he said.

The ringmaster shook his head. ''It isn't guts,'' he said. ''It's patience. I don't rightly know what guts is.''

''I saw the little yellow runt in the tree,'' a soldier was saying. ''He had no gun, not even a grenade, and as I was going to shoot him he starts screaming for mercy. 'Come down, you runt,' I says, but he didn't, and then he starts gettin' cocky, shoutin' 'Banzai! Banzai!', but I soon put a stop to that.''

''I don't rightly know what guts is,'' Morgan Todds was repeating in an even voice. ''It's just that you get to command the cats, and they obey you. Some can, and some can't. Take Pussyfoot Deakin, now. He's a woman, he is. Comes in to me one night when I'm training them. I'd just shut them up. 'It's the ambition of my life,' he says.

'' 'What's the ambition of your life?' I says.

62

" 'To command the cats,' he says. 'That's my ambition.'

" 'Well, command 'em,' I says, and I chucks him the whip.

" 'No,' he says, alarmed like. 'No, don't go. I don't think I could do it. I don't really. It's just that I'd like to.'

" 'It's just that you'd like to,' I mimics. 'It's just that you'd like to.'

"I go to let the cats into the ring, but Deakin slips outside and he's plain scared. Me? I'm wild by now, that sissy thinkin' he c'n do what I'm doing.

" 'You'd like to command the cats, eh?' I says. Then I opened the cages, and out they came. I can tell you by this time I am roaring wild, which is a bad way to be when the cats are loose, because they know, bein' sensitive to atmosphere.

" 'Come on, Jesse,' I says, and I opens the first cage. 'Come on, Pouncer,' I says, and I opens the second cage. 'Out, Pollo,' I says, and then I open the cage for Gouger, and he's the biggest cat and the wildest. The others I have reared from cubs, but he only came to us last year, and a trouble he's been. 'Out, Gouger,' I says, and Gouger comes bounding across, his eyes yellower than his hair.

"Deakin is white now. 'Put 'em back, Mr Todds,' he says; 'put 'em back.'

" 'Come and command them,' I says. Then I begin to yell, and crack the whip so that the cats are runnin', threadin' in and out and beginnin' to snarl.

" 'I don't reckon I can,' he says. 'Course you can't,' I says. 'What about your life's ambition?'

"Deakin is close to shiverin' now. I'm yellin' and crackin' the whip. Gouger is comin' at me all the time, but the other cats are keepin' back.

" 'You want to wear gold braid and ribbon,' I says to Deakin, but I'm not looking at him. 'You want red colour slashed through your strides. Why don't you get a job as the man outside a picture show?' I says, and I cracks the whip so that the cats are snarlin' fearful.

" 'Stop it,' Deakin says. 'They'll get you, Morgan.'

"I saw they were gettin' restless, and Gouger in particular, so I pushed 'em back. Jesse and Pollo and Pouncer were easy. I slammed the doors after they went in, and locked them.

" 'Up, Gouger,' I says. 'Back, Gouger,' but he was restless. He almost gets to the cage when he turns. 'In you go,' I tells him, but he goes in backing, which is bad.

" 'Get in, you yellow rogue!' I says, and cracks the whip. When I get him in I slam the door and go to fasten it. That was when he got me, and in half a minute my hand is a hot, bloody mess; ribbons you might say.

" 'Deakin,' I yells, but Deakin don't answer, and when I look around he's fainted. 'Ruddy sis,' I says, but others are coming. In the hospital the doc says the hand will have to come off."

The smallish man in the worn black clothes was not even excited. His voice was a steady monotone. The six soldiers and Denny were staring at him and the bandaged hand.

" 'Take that off, doc?' I says. 'Don't be mad. I need that hand.'

" 'You'll never tame lions again,' he says.

" 'I don't tame 'em,' I says, 'I command 'em, and I need my hand for that, which means you don't take it off.'

"The doc shakes his head. 'It's got to come off,' he says. 'It's ripped something terrible.'

" 'Ripped or not, it stays on,' I says.

"They didn't take it off, and after a few weeks the doc says maybe a skin graft will do. After the graft I go back to the circus, but no one's been near the cats except to feed 'em, and Gouger is too big and fat for my liking, although some will tell you they're better when they're well fed, which is only partly true. Gouger looks at me, cunning and knowing as any cat. He just looks nasty at me. I have to go on with the act, you know."

One of the soldiers offered Morgan Todds a cigarette, which he took without appearing glad. He lit it and seemed disinclined to say more.

"It must take guts, this lion business," said a soldier.

"Not guts," said Morgan Todds; "patience." He sat awhile, and then pointed to the camped circus. There was no movement in the whole camp except for the flicker of golden fires. "Just listen," he said, "and you'll hear them grunt."

They waited until a lion grunted and another coughed and growled.

"Sounds terrible to you," said Morgan Todds, "but it's nothing to me, because I'm used to it. They require patience and understanding, that's all. Some say you need guts, but, then, what is guts? I don't rightly know.

"I knew a doctor who had guts," he went on. "He was our M.O. in France in 'eighteen. I was in the Flying Corps then, a pilot, when flying wasn't fancy like it is now. We went up in those days first with .45 Colts and later an m.g. strapped on, but any bombs you dropped was over the side. Those were the early days, and you might say a plane wasn't much use like they are today, if you call that sort of thing being useful.

"Our job was mainly shooting Jerries out of the sky, and that was their job, too, so there was fun for all. I scored a few Jerries before they got me, and then I didn't know it. I woke up to find myself in base hospital and our own unit M.O. specially come back to look after me.

" 'We'll get you well, Todds,' he says, 'you're a good pilot.'

"They did, too, because they had the best man possible on the job, a Hun prisoner-of-war. The M.O. tells me about it, and if there is anything our M.O. hated it was Huns.

" 'I hate 'em, Todds,' he says. 'I hate 'em, but he's the only man that can fix you. He says he will have you flying in six weeks. I believe he will, too, but I hate him all the same, because he's a Hun.'

"He had me fixed in about six weeks, too, and there is a plate in my head. The day I'm due to fly the M.O. brings the Jerry surgeon along with him and they watch me go up. When I come down again the M.O. is there with the Hun M.O. Our doc is white, but congratulates me. 'Pretty good, Todds,' he says, 'and the Hun did it all right.'

"He went over to the Hun, then, and he goes to put out his hand. I never thought he could do it, even though that Hun had operated and given me back half a head as you might say. When they got me my brains were half out. You could see them pumping, they told me. That's why I thought a lot of our M.O. as he goes to shake hands with the Hun. Then our M.O. pulls back his hand as though he can't do it after all, and the Jerry is looking at him, puzzled. At last the M.O. shakes hands with him, and the Jerry is beaming all over his face. I reckon that is guts.

" 'That takes guts,' I says to the M.O. .

" 'I'll never get my hand clean for weeks,' the M.O. says."

Morgan Todds looked at Denny and the soldiers. "That's guts for you," he said.

The soldiers nodded.

"I've still got the plate there," said the circus man. He tapped the crown of his head. There may or may not have been a plate there, for all anybody knew.

"So the hand still isn't healed?" said Denny. The soldiers looked at the bandage.

The small man said nothing. He was taking a bottle from one pocket with his good hand. He unstoppered the bottle and began pouring a pale yellow liquid over the bandage, so that the fluid soaked through the cloth. "Antiseptic," he explained. "Keeps it clean." He put the bottle away.

Denny looked at his watch and saw there was an hour to go before the Sydney train arrived. The room was just beginning to warm.

"This is a new wound," said Morgan Todds. There was no expression in his voice, no pride or impatience. "Gouger got me again the night before last. He's had it in for me ever since the day Deakin did his fancy prancin' in front of the cages, and he was able to rip my hand.

"I'd watched that cat, because in forty years no cat has got me beyond a scratch. It's not that I'm losing my nerve, because nerve isn't in it. It's patience you need, and that cat's wearing down my patience. He knew he had to make me wild to get me off my guard, but I was watching.

" 'You don't get me goin', Gouger,' I says, 'I've patience enough for you.' That isn't strictly true, because I'm tired of the game — 'browned off' as you might say; 'had it', as they say in the Army.

"Gouger's waiting for me to change my tactics, but I take him through every night the same. 'Up, Gouger,' I says. 'Down, Gouger,' I says. 'Back, boy,' I says, and it is after that he slashed at me. Thought he had me then, but quick as lightning I switch the whip across and in two jiffs I have him in the cage, and both he and me are surprised.'

" 'You big yeller cat,' I says, 'you're in there again.'

"Gouger glares at me, but he knows he's beaten for the time. We're both wonderin' about next time.''

Morgan Todds had finished his cigarette and was huddled into a dark sombre shape upon his chair.

"Tonight," he went on, "I had the cats out, and there was something different about everything. The crowds roared as they always do, and they were just faces, and the cats were there, roaring and growling, so that the crowd was scared and liking it, and I wasn't scared and still not liking it. I was tired, I tell you, and I knew the cats was watching me. I played with the other cats, and then let Gouger out. I knew he couldn't break my patience, not when I was tired like I was.

"When he came out he was growling and prowling, and I whipped the other cats back, and played with him. Then he smelt the blood beneath the bandage, and he kept getting worked up, and all the time I knew he might do something he'd never done before. You can't fathom cats when there's the smell of blood, and it's your blood. He keeps edging near me, but he knows I'm not flustered but that I'm tired enough to watch every move, and never lose me block.

"His eyes are glaring yellow, and his big head has the hair standing out round it. After that I put him back into the cage, and he goes, hatin' it, and me, but goin' back all the same. Yes, he went back.''

Morgan Todds diminished, and was only a small tired man upon a waiting-room chair. One hand held the other bandaged one. The fire began to sink in the room, and Denny knew the train would be in soon.

"Forty years I've had," said Morgan Todds, "forty years, and it's too much for a man. I'm gettin' out of the game, soon as I can. I shouldn't be surprised how soon.''

He looked at the six soldiers and Denny. "No," he said. "I shouldn't be surprised how soon. I might even leave tonight, and never come back.''

MR
HICKEN'S
PEARS

Mr Hicken was a man inclined to talk to himself quite a lot. The Wirril Creek people often saw him talking, either to himself or the flowers in his front garden.

Perhaps he talked to himself because there was little he could see, so that he liked to hear sounds — the sound of his own voice, the singing hum of the bees in the flowers, and the rustle of the pear tree, right up against his own window, its leaves upon the hard glass. And especially in the winter he liked to hear its thousand brown leaves bouncing and scraping across the house paddock.

If there was a thing he loved more than hearing sounds, it was smelling smells. Take the pear trees, for example. Mr Hicken liked the smell of pears, and the riper the better. Also his plums, peaches and nectarines. In all Wirril Creek there were not peaches, plums and nectarines like Mr Hicken's.

Often the locals would see him gazing down at this great heap of fallen fruit, shaking his head, sadly or happily they would not know, but shaking his head all the same, and talking, perhaps to the clumped, droning masses of bees, taking sweetness from the old man's fruit. The locals hated to see all that fruit going to waste, rotting, as it were, on the ground.

"Mr Hicken," they would say, "you have a lot of fruit there."

Mr Hicken would nod, peer towards where the voice was, and say, "A lot of fruit, all right."

"Fly, eh?" they would say. "Fly bad this year?"

"Flies? Yes, they're bad enough," Mr Hicken would say. "Sticky this year."

"Fruit-fly," they would explain. "Fly got into the fruit, eh?"

"Go on," Mr Hicken would say, slightly interested. Mr Hicken would never have been able to see even one fly.

"Pity," they would say, "pity about the fly."

Mr Hicken never caught on. He never told them to come in and take what they wished to take. Instead he let the heaped fruit rot, taking his delight in the visiting bees, for he loved their droning sound. Rarely he ate a single peach or nectarine, so that his orchard was a fruit-fly's paradise.

The pears, above all, were the envy of all Wirril Creek. Given half a chance all the Wirril Creek housewives would have been into his orchard quickly as a shot out of a gun, their sugar bags loaded, and out again. There were other pear trees in Wirril Creek, but they suffered badly from the depredations of the flying-foxes. Shrieking and quarrelling all night, those great flapping creatures would ruin the crop before it ripened, that is, excepting Mr Hicken's fruit.

Why the flying-foxes should not choose to attack the succulent pears of Mr Hicken had always been a problem unsolved, to the folk of Wirril Creek. Pears are pears, wherever they are, and flying-foxes are not given to whims and fancies, especially where pears are large and golden. There was some tale concerning Mr Hicken, who, in the days before his son Ralph went away to enlist, would stand every night on his back doorstep and swear at the flying animals. Much as this said for Mr Hicken's ability to swear, the tale is probably overrated.

Some had it that Mr Hicken would bang a large gong, persistently, whilst others had it he waved a golden lamp. Whatever he did, or did not do, the foxes, as far back as most could remember, had never landed on the magic pear tree.

That Saturday morning, then, when Mr Hicken stood beneath his pear tree surveying a pile of saffron fruit, tears dropped from his eyes. They may have been tears of joy, for Mr Hicken seemed to feel things very much.

Whenever he "felt", moisture would gather in his dim eyes,

so that when he shook his head, out of sheer excess of feeling, the tears dropped. Now those tears were falling on the ripened fruit. Mr Hicken loved those pears.

When he heard the harsh dry scraping of a dray, and the dull thumping of a horse's hooves, he did not look up. He muttered on to his pears. When he was hailed, however, he paused a moment, and ceased from contemplating his fruit.

"Ah, there, Mr Hicken!" said a voice, a bright, cheery kind of voice.

Mr Hicken peered, but could not see. He shook his head. "Snapjacks, watermelons, peanuts and squash!" said the voice.

Mr Hicken shook his head in bewilderment. It all meant nothing to him.

"Cheap!" said the voice. "Cheapest in Wirril Creek."

"Ah," said Mr Hicken. He made his way towards the voice. The word "cheap" excited him somewhat, for Mr Hicken had the reputation of being "close". He wanted to see what was cheap.

When he got to the dray he saw, dimly, two boys seated just in rear of the horse's rump. One was young Jim Hickey, Dolly Hickey's boy, as he could see, bright-faced, merry, with impudent eyes, and a flat squash in his hands. The other boy, bullet-headed, he did not know. This boy stared at him, for it was the first time in his life he had seen Mr Hicken and he was intrigued, especially by the manner in which Mr Hicken's hair, for all its age, came looping down over his forehead, almost to the long-pointed nose beneath the dimmed watery eyes. Nevertheless he nodded and said, " 'Morning, Mr Hicken.''

Mr Hicken nodded. He kept staring at the squash. "I can't grow stuff like that," he said. "Can't grow a thing."

"Watermelons," said the Hickey boy proudly. "Can't beat them for size."

"Can't grow watermelons," grumbled Mr Hicken. "Can't grow anything."

Dolly Hickey's boy was no fool. Also, he was out for business. "Grow anything on your place, Mr Hicken," he

70

said, waving a hand across two hundred green acres, ''and look at your fruit trees.''

''Fruit grows without water,'' said Mr Hicken irritably. ''Can't grow anything else without water.'' He shook his head.

''Cheap they are,'' said the small salesman. ''Bob the watermelons. Zac the squash and snapjacks. Peanuts bob a pound.''

''Ah,'' said Mr Hicken, ''Peanuts.'' His eyes, if it was possible, gleamed. Mr Hicken had always wanted to grow peanuts. That he could not grow them rankled him, somewhere inside.

''Can't grow 'em,'' said Mr Hicken. ''Never have been able to.''

Dolly Hickey's boy had almost forgotten Mr Hicken. He was gazing wistfully at the tree of golden pears. It was not that he liked china-pears himself, not to speak of, anyway. His bright little mind was thinking of all the needful wives of Wirril Creek, they with their preserving pans put away, their sugar unused, their bottles empty; for when peaches and apricots are bottled, what else is there to preserve but the pears that the flying-foxes have eaten?

The Hickey boy could see, as in a dream, his dray filled with pears, golden pears that heaped up, high, that smelled sweetly beneath his nostrils, that tumbled from his dray, so many he had of them. He could even hear his own voice shouting, ''Pears! Good yeller pears! Mr Hicken's good yeller pears!''

In this dream he could see the good wives of Wirril Creek, flowing from every house and home, they with their baskets and their dishes, all descending on him for his pears. They were thanking him, and he was asking almost any money, and getting it.

Mr Hicken was feeling. Tears gathered in his eyes, rheumed their way down his face. A red hairy paw wiped them away. ''Peanuts,'' he said sadly.

''You c'd grow them,'' said the bullet-headed boy.

''And when Ralph comes home he won't stay. That's certain,'' said Mr Hicken.

71

"Ah, Ralph coming home?" said the Hickey boy, interestedly.

"Coming home, and he won't stay," said Mr Hicken.
"Ralph said more'n once that he wouldn't farm where there
was no water." He shook his head sadly. "He won't either,"
he said.

"Well, then," said the Hickey boy, "you've got to have
water."

The old man shook his head. "No water," he mumbled.
These youngsters talked a lot; more than in his day. No water,
no Ralph. He could see Ralph, home for a day, or a week
perhaps, but not after that. No water.

"Coming back from the islands he won't want to stay," he
said. It was just now a man wanted his boy with him. His eyes
moistened.

The boy Hickey could see Ralph coming home, tall, thin,
misty, a kitbag over his shoulder, a samurai sword at his side,
and perhaps, like Sam Lonegan, with a few grass skirts for the
girls to giggle over. He could see Ralph looking about for water
and finding none and, disgusted, leaving the old man to mumble
to his pears. No, that would be a bad thing. Also the Hickey
boy was wanting his dray filled with pears.

Leaning down from his seat, his head cupped in his hands, his
brown eyes earnest, the Hickey boy said to Mr Hicken, "Just
where is the water you have got, Mr Hicken?"

"Not enough. Not enough," said Mr Hicken. "A spoonful,
no more, you might say."

"Then show it to us," said the bullet-headed boy, "and we
might be able to do something."

Mr Hicken shook his head. Boys, boys, boys. He wanted to
get back to his pears. He wanted to grow peanuts. He did not
want boys. Nevertheless he took them through the wicket-gate,
leading them past the rotting fruit, the luscious pears, until they
were in his fields of green paspalum. Red cows stared at them,
but he led the boys past the stock until they stood on the edge of
a ridge, the edge itself cupped somewhat, and gapped in a small

cleft, about eight feet high. Through the dip trickled a stream of clear water. It glittered in the new sunlight, gurgling as it was lost between rocks, finally disappearing over the ridge.

"That's all," said Mr Hicken. "That's the lot. Not another creek." He waved his hand across the green acres. "Not another creek," he said. "No rain and it'll all look dry." He shook his head. "Not enough for Ralph." He gazed sadly into distance.

The Hickey boy and his bullet-headed companion exchanged stares. "Easy," they said, together.

Mr Hicken was shaking his head. He wished, now, they would go. He was tired of them.

"You've just got to dam it," said the Hickey boy. "Dam it on the edge of the ridge, and you've got all the water you want."

"Eh?" said Mr Hicken.

"There." The boys pointed to the edge of the ridge. "Dam that and you'll have plenty of water."

"Well, now," said Mr Hicken. His face began to shine. "Dam it, eh?" Then he shook his head. "Couldn't dam it."

"Yes," said the boys, "easily."

"Nothing to dam it with," said Mr Hicken. His eyes were beginning to moisten again. Excitement was telling on him.

"There's a ton of rock there," said the Hickey boy, "and I've got the dray, see? I can get some stuff in it, see?"

"Do it easily," said the boy with the bullet-shaped head. He looked serious and confident.

"Well, bless my soul!" said Mr Hicken.

After that he did not argue. He let them go their way. There was, on his part, much shaking of the head. He was sure Ralph would not stay. The boy had said the place was no good without water, too risky. No, he could not believe all this about the dam.

The boys decided the rocks were not enough so they went away. He heard his front rails clatter to the ground, and the dray scrape away. The boys were away a long time, and when they came back again he had dreamed the dam into, and out of, existence. They had rocks in their dray, which they unloaded.

They went away, again, the dray wheels scraping against the loose brake leathers.

They returned with a dray-load of yellow clay, and on the top two shovels sticking up, triumphantly. Mr Hicken thought they must have been his own shovels.

"Bless my soul!" said Mr Hicken, again, when he saw the load they had.

The boys began stacking the rock against the edge of the cleft in the ridge. There was cunning in every stone laid. The small trickle began to swell as it was pressed back in the hollow.

Said Mr Hicken, for the third time, "Bless my soul!" This time he said it delightedly.

He sat down on the bank, and took off his boots. He removed his thick black socks, baring his white feet. Then he rolled up his trousers, almost to the knees. His white legs had few hairs on them. Next he ventured into the water.

The water was cool, but soft. It spread, at first, about Mr Hicken's toes, seemed to gurgle delightedly at making the old man's acquaintance, and bid him venture further.

With a curious feeling at his heart Mr Hicken did so. He waded until he was ankle-deep, and all the time his eyes were tearful; with joy this time.

"I believe we will do it, boys," he said.

The boys nodded, for they were very busy. Time and again they had played at this in the creek and they knew their game well. Mr Hicken watched them, happy and amazed. He even began to pick up rocks, and pass them to the boys. Each rock the boys acknowledged, as though Mr Hicken's rocks were important above other rocks. This pleased Mr Hicken, who, after a time, began to direct things, although more or less apologetically.

"Now look, boys, don't you think that rock ought to go there?" he would say, pointing.

"Why, of course, Mr Hicken." And the rock would be placed there all right, although it is doubtful whether or not Mr Hicken, because of his short-sightedness, saw the winks that were sometimes exchanged.

When the water became knee-deep Mr Hicken had to roll his trousers up along his thin thighs. This he did with pleasure. All the time the wall of the dam was heightening, rocks and yellow clay pugged between them. Mr Hicken could scarcely believe it all.

"Why," he said after a time, "the water'll be over our heads when it fills up."

The boys nodded solemnly. "You can irrigate, then," said the bullet-headed boy, "like Sam Lonegan does."

"But that isn't my land, below," said Mr Hicken. He was wishing now that it was.

"Irrigate back there," said the boy with a jerk of his thumb towards the slight slope of the hill. "Get an engine and a pump and some piping, like Sam Lonegan has."

Mr Hicken shook his head, sadly. "All costs money," he said. He was a trifle irritated by the constant references to Sam Lonegan.

The Hickey boy said, "Ralph could buy it all from his deferred pay. That's how Sam Lonegan bought his."

"Ah," said Mr Hicken. He no longer hated Sam Lonegan. Perhaps there was something in it, Ralph and his deferred pay. If he could get the boy to spend it then he might stay.

"Grow anything then, Mr Hicken," said Dolly Hickey's boy. "Squash, watermelons, rockmelons, peanuts."

"Ah," said Mr Hicken, again. His eyes were beginning to moisten. He could see, clearly enough in his mind, the green lines of the peanut plants on the red turned soil; could smell the spray as he had often smelled rain; and he could see the rich crop of melons, pumpkins and the like. Yes, it would be good if Ralph were to spend his deferred pay.

"I'll buy some of your stuff, now," he said. "I'll buy a squash and some peanuts. How much did you say they were?"

"Peanuts a bob," said the Hickey boy. "Squashes a zac."

"I'll buy a watermelon, too," said Mr Hicken. Mr Hicken, who rarely ate fruit, loved the soft sweetness of watermelon.

The dam was finished. The gurgling had stopped, swallowed up in the swelling volume of water. It almost terrified Mr

Hicken, so much it was after so little. He shook his head so that his hair looped more than ever, and a few tears dripped to his feet.

"Wonderful," he said, "wonderful!"

"Not at all, Mr Hicken," said the Hickey boy. "Only too pleased to do it for you."

Mr Hicken suddenly became aware that the boys had worked for him. They would want money, of course.

They might want a lot of pay. Then there were the vegetables he had promised to buy. A small thrill of terror went through the old man. He looked at the dam, the water of which seemed to increase amazingly in volume before his eyes. He felt uneasy. His eyes, again, began to water.

"Ha," he said nervously. "Well, you'll be going, eh?"

The boys stood silent. Mr Hicken began to feel a sort of terror for the money they might ask. What could he do then, if they asked a high price? He began to wonder whether he should have let them build the dam.

"Mr Hicken," said the Hickey boy seriously, "I was wondering if you'd let us have some pears?"

"Ah," said Mr Hicken. He bent forward as though he might not be able to see the boy.

"We built the dam," said the bullet-headed boy.

"Of course. Of course," said Mr Hicken hurriedly.

"Then we thought . . ." said Dolly Hickey's boy.

"Quite," said Mr Hicken. He gazed wistfully at the golden fruit. "Take what you like," he said in a voice he did not quite recognise as his own. "As much as you wish," he added valiantly.

The boys did not wait to be further urged. They drew their now-empty cart under the magic tree and dropped the ripe fruit into it, Jim Hickey sitting up in the loaded branches and throwing the fruit down to the bullet-headed boy. Mr Hicken scarcely noticed them. He was staring down the paddock at the sheet of water growing before his eyes. He was shaking his head all the time.

When the boys were leaving, their dray filled to capacity as a dream that has come true, golden pears piled high and tumbling, he saw the melons, the peanuts and the squashes lying beneath the tree.

"You've left the vegetables behind," he shouted to them.

"We'll be back," they shouted in reply, "after we get the next load."

Mr Hicken nodded. Perhaps they would give him two squashes, and not even charge him; or, anyway, give him an extra pound of peanuts. Yes, he'd prefer an extra pound of peanuts, although soon he'd be growing his own. He chuckled over that, his head bending lower.

At first he was thinking about the water in the dam, then the irrigation, then Ralph and his coming home, and his deferred pay.

The two boys looked back and saw him staring down at the heaped pears.

"He's talking to himself," they said. Nevertheless they rather liked the picture of the old man, standing there, his head bent, looking down at the golden fruit. Because they were a good distance away and the wheels scraped on the brake leathers, they could not hear his chuckle.

THE
SONS
OF
NIM

Nim Thorgood was a small brightly black-eyed Norwegian, and it was a pity he ever died.

The Coolbucca people were sure that they hadn't recently received fuel anything like the bloodwood and tallowwood blocks Nim supplied. Twenty miles he carted it, charging seven shillings for a piled dray-load. There are many tales told about Nim and his sawn blocks, and how he always demanded cash, and how the then Mayor of Coolbucca, Mr James Portland, had had a load delivered, and after inspecting the load had pronounced himself satisfied.

"Very good, my man," he said. "I shall order more, I think."

Nim Thorgood, who seemed not to have absorbed this latter information, held out his hand for the cash.

"Ah, yes," said Mr Portland. "Send the bill in. I pay accounts monthly." He then went on speaking to a councillor, and completely ignored Nim.

Nim began loading the blocks on to his dray. "No monthly. She ain't monthly," he was saying to himself. Mr James Portland looked around and saw with dismay that he was losing his load.

"Hey!" he shouted.

"She ain't monthly," said Nim. He threw some more blocks on the dray to prove that.

"Now look here," said Mayor Portland, who had never been refused a monthly, or even a six-monthly, consideration. "Look here, old chap!"

"Ain't no monthly," said Nim. And a few more blocks

78

went on, after which the Mayor parted with seven shillings and a small amount of dignity. Nim always exacted immediate payment.

Nim had started with an axe, a crosscut saw and a wife, all Norwegian. After a time he bought an engine, and set up a sawbench. The engine, when it came, was drawn from nowhere by three large draughts, and seemed a burden for them. When Nim started it up everyone voted him either a very brave or foolish man, and the crowd which came to watch regarded the phenomenon from a safe distance, which was considered to be about four hundred yards, and when it began puffing and blowing they retreated even further than that, and when, finally, Nim decided to let off steam, or rather to allow the engine to do so, then every cow in Garland's Point and environs gathered its udder and ran, and worn-out draughts kicked up their heels and went careering across the stumped paddocks.

Nim made history with that engine and his circular-saw. He cut more wood than he carted, and many said he would have had that amount again were the engine not so avaricious, but Nim seemed not to mind, and gave himself to sawing more, and carting more, whilst his wife hurriedly gave birth to children, five sons, who in no time appeared to be as tall as their small father.

Sach was the eldest, and then Lash, and when Sach was ready to work he decided that milled timber might be a good thing, and told his father so. Nim, when he had allowed the idea to sink in, became quite excited and rushed off to Sydney to buy a new machine. The great iron-clad puffing-billy drove the new machine, and they had sawn timber for housing.

This enabled Nim to put skillions on the northern, the eastern and the southern sides of the original building he had constructed for his wife and the children, so that there was no longer any overcrowding, even if the house appeared to ramble somewhat. Nim could not help admiring his own handiwork, and would often look up from his sawing and spend a few moments in contemplation. For the most part, however, he continued to saw blockwood, and allow Sach to mill the other timber.

When Lash was able to partner Sach he suggested a machine for dressing the timber, and Nim, again excited, went to Sydney. After that the district was well supplied with slabs, sawn and dressed, and dressed strips to nail over the cracks where the slabs had shrunk.

When Noll came along he proved to be somewhat of a mechanic, so that they were able to fix their own machines and save money on maintenance. The main thing about Noll, however, apart from his work, was his violin. Somehow he had shown an aptitude for this instrument, had been trained in its use, and was capable of producing the most unusual music from its strings. Nim, alone, recognised the Norwegian in the boy, although he said nothing about that. He allowed Noll to play for the dances at the Garland's Point hall, but mostly Noll played for the family, in the big central room where the meals were cooked, where they ate and lived and entertained.

There Noll would play, and Nim, listening, would be reminded of his own Norway by the sea, and all that it meant, and after Noll had finished his playing Nim would tell the family various old tales, in which they appeared to take only a polite and casual interest.

After Noll there were Lars and Sammy. They were just two more like the others, short spare men, with no backside to speak of, dropping in a straight line from shoulders to heels, and tapered a little, so that they appeared to be much the same when viewed from front, sides or rear.

The Thorgoods, then, were a united family, with the mill as their central pivot-point, and labour in it their delight. If there was any difference anywhere among the boys it existed in Sammy, who was the youngest, and for whom the entire family maintained a special affection. Sammy worked as hard as the other brothers when it came to his time to work, but he was allowed a skillion all on his own, whereas the other brothers were forced to share, and Sammy, in some way, did seem a trifle different, although he was not anxious to emphasise differences, but clung, strongly, to a sameness.

It was when old Nim died that Sammy showed the difference. He wept where the others were simply solemn, and at the funeral cried incessantly ''Daddy! Daddy!'' whereas the boys, and even their mother, seemed more bewildered than sorry, as though they dimly felt that they would miss old Nim and his dray with the careful mixture of bloodwood and tallowwood blocks. Nim always strongly asserted that tallowwood and bloodwood were made to burn together.

After Nim died the Second World War broke out, and the boys, having grown sufficiently by that time, were eligible for it, although they did not immediately enlist. It took quite some time for enthusiasm to filter through to Garland's Point, and then another period of time elapsed before that enthusiasm penetrated the roar and whistling of the mill. And it was not until the Lanyon brothers enlisted — three in all — and there was a patriotic meeting called at Coolbucca and two boys from Wirril Creek joined the Army that the Thorgoods really knew there was a war on.

At about that time the invasion of Norway was quickly accomplished, much to the indignation of the old Thorgood woman, who immediately insisted that the boys go across to Europe and do something. Nothing loth, Sach enlisted, but he demanded that only Lash might enlist with him, for, apart from Norway, the mill was what counted. Noll, however, overrode Sach and enlisted with him, so that that meant three Thorgoods in the Army, and Mrs Thorgood relaxed somewhat, feeling that Norway was in good hands, whilst the mill might easily be run by Lars and Sammy.

After a time Lars became morose, and nothing less than the Airforce would please him. Sammy said it was no use one working a mill, and that, anyway, he just couldn't manage it, and he revealed to his mother that Norway was what he was worried about, and this pleased the old woman immensely, so that she consented to be left on her own, and with no sons to look after she took care of the mill. Sach, however, did not allow his mother to remain long alone, for one weekend he brought home a wife, a Sydney girl who was, nevertheless, sensible. She took up the northern skillion.

Lash, home on leave, decided to marry a Garland's Point girl, a sister of Alan Lanyon, who was in his battalion. She took the eastern skillion and kept Mrs Thorgood, senior, and the other Mrs Thorgood company. Then the boys went overseas, much to the old woman's relief, as she had not ceased thinking about Norway's plight.

Sammy wrote no word home, and it was fully six months before they found out that he was in the Merchant Navy. This was not, perhaps, considered to be a fighting force, but it was the next thing to it, and Mrs Thorgood was satisfied. She superintended the weekly oiling of machines, remembering the roar and the noise of the mill in its working days, and hoped all her boys would return.

The news filtered through that Noll had been promoted to an entertainment group, but it was to be understood that he, Noll, would be in the fighting when it came along, or, as he said, he'd be there when the whips were cracking. Army, Airforce and Merchant Navy; Mrs Thorgood was puzzled about the delayed release of Norway. She thought, perhaps, that insufficient notice had been taken of her boys, and that they had been held back, through jealousy, from launching a quick and effective campaign. She was puzzled when the boys returned from England and the Middle East, but accepted the fact calmly, and even, some time later, the birth of a son to Sach, and a son also to Lash.

Then the war came to a conclusion, and after a while the boys returned; that is, with the exception of Sammy, who had either been killed or was detained in the Merchant Navy. The welcome-home dance to the Thorgoods was a terrific affair, everyone in the district turning up, especially the girls, who admired Lars in his blue uniform and adored Noll's playing. Some said Noll would be a fool to go back to the mill when he could play like that. "Divine," most of the girls called it, and there were not a few who looked knowing, as though they had discovered a genius in Noll, unbeknown to Noll. But since they were unable or reluctant to contact someone great who would recognise Noll he returned to the mill with the three brothers, and very hard they worked to restore it and the trade they had lost through the war period.

Their mill whistle shrieked in the morning, and in the

evening at knock-off time, and everyone set his watch by it. Many were the bullockies who hauled their great logs, and when petrol became more available the log-lorries groaned beneath the beloved tallowwood of old Nim, and red and white mahogany for the post-war building. The Thorgood boys delighted in the orders which they were unable to fulfil. They employed hands, and began work themselves before the hands, and knocked off after the hands. Sach went to Sydney and bought new and better machines, and timber was trucked to Sydney and all over Australia to build new homes.

Sach built a skillion onto his skillion, and Lash followed suit, and after a time Noll and Lars both decided to marry, so that skillions had to be added to their skillions, and old Nim's house rambled even more, and still Sammy did not return. They had heard from him, but not enough, for Sammy was a close one. Old Mrs Thorgood was of the opinion "that the sea had got him", which did not mean he was drowned, but that there was a something in his blood that enabled the sea to be his mistress. Sach would not have that, and the other brothers loyally supported him, but the old woman continued her muttering.

After a time Sammy returned. Apprehensive, the brothers expected him to have changed, but he was the same Sammy, only, perhaps, a trifle more thoughtful.

He appeared very much to enjoy the welcome-home, especially the dance part of it, when there was much merriment and kind attention by the Garland's Point girls, who felt Sammy's homecoming to be even more romantic than that of his brothers. Everyone wanted to know what Sammy would do, at which Sammy looked surprised and said he was going back to the mill, of course, although Sach, looking at him, was not too happy about Sammy, and didn't think he would stay long.

Sammy, however, did stay, and if differences existed between him and his brothers, and it seemed a pity Sammy didn't marry and have children running about in the various skillions, Sammy nonetheless stuck to his special skillion, the western one, which had been built for him when he returned. Sach, who wished Sammy to be married, gave it out that a new house would be built for Sammy when he was married, as the skillions were becoming too many. Sach thought, also, that this would be an incentive for the Garland's Point girls, although they needed little incentive in that respect. No, Sammy seemed scarcely to see the Garland's Point girls, although he was pleasant enough, and after a time the matter of marriage was dropped.

Sammy, however, appeared to grow more thoughtful as the days passed, and this disturbed Sach, for he could not contemplate Sammy leaving, or even tolerate that thought. He even urged Sammy to take a trip to Sydney thinking Sammy might find a wife there, and Sammy went to Sydney, just to please Sach, but when he returned it was without a wife.

Then Sammy told the brothers he was going. ''Going?'' Sach said. He shook his head in disappointment.

''What you say, Sammy?'' said Noll. ''You can't go, Sammy.''

''I want to go,'' Sammy said miserably.

''The sea's got him,'' his mother said, as though she knew the sea might get all Norwegians, even small black-eyed Norwegians like Sammy.

''It ain't the sea,'' said Sammy slowly. The old woman took no notice, but continued her muttering.

''I'll build you a new home, there,'' said Sach. ''Get a wife and settle down. You can't beat a mill.''

''A new home'd be very nice,'' said Sammy. ''But I want to go back to the sea.''

''Said it was the sea,'' the old woman chuckled scornfully, but the boys were too worried about Sammy to listen to her.

Their efforts to both retain Sammy and find him a wife redoubled. Noll made Sammy accompany him with the orchestra in which he played. The orchestra, so-called, was really a dance-band, and played at most local dances. Sammy went with Noll, and was introduced to quite an assortment of girls, but none seemed to take his eye. He seemed more interested in Noll's playing of the violin, and indeed while Noll played he would never shift his attention. Noll's playing appeared to fascinate him. It made him even more thoughtful, and next day, after the playing, he would continue to be thoughtful.

One night he told the family he was going the next day. That shocked them.

"Going, Sammy?" Sach said. "But where?"

"Norway," said Sammy.

"Norway?" they all said. Old Mrs Thorgood appeared to be very excited. She forgot to speak Australian. Sammy would not say why he was going to Norway.

"Norway?" the old woman said excitedly. "What you go there for, Sammy?"

"Oh, just go," said Sammy.

Sach wasn't content with that. "What for, Sammy?" he asked.

"I'll get married," Sammy said, and his voice was almost surly.

"Married!" The family was excited, but not happily so.

"Plenty of women here," Lash said.

"Or in Sydney," said Sach, looking at his wife.

"Or here," said Lars, looking at his.

Mrs Thorgood mumbled something which none appeared to hear.

All the brothers sighed. They gave Sammy up. Noll went to get his violin, and when he played it was the curious music of his childhood when old Nim listened and nodded and nodded and listened, and for a time it seemed that old Nim was with them again, nodding and listening. They remembered the solemn tales Nim told, and after a while they thought Sammy must be very different, and probably it was quite right his going home to Norway to live.

When Noll finished the playing Sammy said he thought he would go tomorrow all right, but the brothers wanted him to stay another day at least so that they could fix up a farewell. Sammy agreed, and the brothers fixed the farewell properly. There was a dance at the hall, and the news, flying quickly, brought all the local folk, especially the girls, who thought they'd have a last try. Sach had bought a keg, and to this keg the brothers, Sammy included, went for comfort during the night, having recourse to it many times. After a time Noll gave it out that he was going to play his violin out of the orchestra, which he did, and the girls all vowed Noll had never played so beautifully, and those who knew shook their heads mysteriously, and said it was a pity Noll didn't do something with that talent. But Noll was trying to do something with it, so sadly, so sweetly, so fiercely he played in a vain endeavour to keep his brother Sammy in the family, and with it. But the sweeter, the sadder, the fiercer the music, the more did Sammy wish to go to Norway.

Noll came down to the keg, and after a time wished to play again, but by this time the dance had finished and all had gone with the exception of the five Thorgood boys, who insisted they would never go home. They sat in the rich darkness, and Noll played and the small men wept together, and in that state Sammy said he'd never leave them if he could help it, and they took this to be a sort of promise, so that they wept again, and Noll insisted on playing more music. But so uninhibited was he with the releasing action of the drink that he played weirdly and beautifully, and made Sammy want to rise on certain wings and flee to Norway without having to work his passage in some bitch of a tramp.

They all went home to their skillions, and Sammy slept on the floor in the living-room. He knew they would use his skillion when he left it, and was rather glad. He worked next day until three in the afternoon, and then went inside to wash. His brothers, who thought, perhaps, that Sammy's promise of the night before meant something, said nothing, but continued working. Lars, after a time, said he would see Sammy off, and it was generally accepted that Sammy was going, and that was that. They did not regret the dance or the keg.

Sammy said goodbye to them all quietly, and Lars drove him to the station. He watched the dusty road ahead, accelerating in places to make the passage over the corrugations reasonably smooth. "You like Norway, Sammy?" he asked.

"Oh, fair enough," said Sammy.

"You'll stay there?" asked Lars.

"M'm," said Sammy doubtfully.

"Girl, eh?" said Lars.

"Lovely," said Sammy suddenly. "Saw her in Oslo." His words seemed to pour as he described her. "I'll find her," he said enthusiastically.

"Engaged?" said Lars.

Sammy chuckled. "Cut it out, Lars," he said.

They had reached the station. The train wasn't immediately due. Sammy bought his ticket, a single to Sydney. "I'll get a ship in Sydney. Work my way."

"But this girl," said Lars. "What's her name?"

"Don't know," said Sammy. "She was in Oslo. I'll find her again."

"But she might be married," said Lars. "You never know."

"She ain't married," said Sammy confidently. "I'll find her somehow."

Lars shook his head doubtfully, and said "Fancy that." He was still mumbling about it when the Sydney express came churning in. He helped Sammy to a window-seat, and Sammy leaned out, talking until the train went.

As the train gathered up its loins, its clinking, clankering loins, Lars shouted, "Well, come back," thinking that Sammy never would. Sammy, leaning out further, shouted, "I might," but Lars did not appear to have heard, for he was standing, shaking his head, and looking down at the platform. Sammy, in the train, felt suddenly released from the strange family which was his, and Noll's accursed violin, and so free did he feel that he thought he might come back. He turned to Lars to say so a second time, but Lars was lost to him, and the shout that came back to Lars was muffled in sound and the black smoke that rushed away from the engine, so Sammy just waved and waved until Lars and the station were well out of sight.

DOLLY

"What do you reckon's coming, Dad?" says Jim Reggin, and Mr Reggin's blessed if he knows.

A clinking and a rattling, a sweet music of harness, a nodding of a great draught's head, and the man walking beside it is also nodding his head. Clink and a rattle and then silence as the two draw up before the cyclone gate.

"It's old Hicken, begod," says Pat, who is "old" himself if it comes to that.

"Well, fancy, old Hicken, eh?" says Jim as though it must be strange if his father sees it that way.

"Comes to see you once in a blue moon," says Pat, who, anyway, never goes to visit Mr Hicken. "Wonder what he's got?"

Jim thinks that is fairly obvious, but he knows Pat is wondering what might be wrong with the horse.

They see it is a mare, a fine stamp of a beast, fat as butter, bull-necked, high-arched on the rump, and walking with sure tread.

"Fancy old Hicken with that, eh?" says Pat as though Mr Hicken possessing a fine mare passes understanding.

When Mr Hicken arrives he halts a moment, and all the clink and rattling ceases while he wipes sweat from his forehead and deliberately throws it to the ground.

"Hot," says Mr Hicken, standing still and gazing about at the heat.

"Hot, all right," says Pat. "Hot as we've had this summer."

"Yes," says Mr Hicken. He peers towards Mr Reggin. "Pat, isn't it?"

"And Harry Hicken, eh?" says Pat. "Years since I saw you."

"Years," agrees Mr Hicken excitedly. "Years it is. I was saying to myself this morning, 'It's years since I saw old Pat.' Lord, the times we used to see each other in those days, and now we never have a sight of one another. Yes, it's a long time, all right."

"Nice sort of a mare you've got there," says Pat.

"Like it, eh?"

"Ye-es," says Pat conservatively. "It's all right to *look* at."

"Ah," says Mr Hicken. He snuffles through his nose, wipes it with the back of his hand, looks lovingly at the mare, fondles it about the neck.

"Good old Dolly," he says.

He turns to Pat. "I've worked her," he says, as though it is something to have done that. "You mightn't think so, but I've worked her."

"Work all right, eh?" shouts Pat.

"Yes," says Mr Hicken mildly. "Works all right. Bit fast. Bit too fast."

"No good for you," says Pat, still talking loudly. "Fast mare no good for you." It has suddenly struck Mr Reggin that perhaps Mr Hicken wishes to sell his mare.

"Too fast, all right," mumbles Mr Hicken, but then turns severely to his neighbour. "Mind you," he maintains, "for a man who can work a fast horse there is nothing better. Gets through the work, she does." He pauses a moment, looking into the spaces of Wirril Creek, calmly into the valley, contemplatively towards the hill. "I says to myself, I says, that if I can find a man who can work her, then I've got a buyer."

"Ah," says Pat, and he gives Jim a wink.

"And," says Mr Hicken, wagging a finger at Pat Reggin, "I hear then that your horse foundered last week and died on you."

"Not it," says Pat in answer to the first part of the statement. "No horse of mine ever foundered. Twisted gut it was. Twisted in the bowel. You can't do nothing about that."

"Twisted, eh?" says Mr Hicken, who appears only to have heard the one word.

Pat Reggin seats himself comfortably against the split fence and Jim, who knows the signs, also makes himself comfortable, drawing a paspalum stalk on which to bite, but Mr Hicken remains standing, holding the winkers, leaning slightly against the mare. He realises, perhaps, that in a lifetime one may only have one animal which dies from a twisted bowel, and he understands that a man would wish to speak about it.

"Saturday night," says Mr Reggin, "I saw that horse as good as you or me. Baldy — that's her mate, the chestnut — he comes up to the fence on his side, and she comes up on her side, and they sniff each other, and Baldy walks off and never comes near again, for surely to God they both knew there was something wrong. Human it was. Next morning Biddy's sitting on her haunches like a dog, and sick — you never seen the like of it. Jim here gives her a dose, but I tell Jim she's past a drench. And," says Pat with lugubrious triumph, "she is, too. Vet says it's no good after they sit up."

"No!" says Mr Hicken with violent emphasis. Then he shakes his head sadly for poor Biddy sitting up past all hope of drenching.

"Then next day she dies," says Pat sorrowfully. "Best worker I ever had, although, mind you, she were a fair bitch to break in. Stubborn."

"Hard to break in, eh?"

"Just when she was needed, too," says Pat ruminatively. "Threw up her legs, then drew them in. Died of cramps, really."

"Terrible," says Mr Hicken, shaking his head and seeing Biddy die of the cramps.

"The vet says she never had no chance," says Pat. "He says you can't do nothing for a twisted gut."

"Ah, well," says Mr Hicken.

He looks directly at Pat. "I thought," he says, "that you would be wanting a mare. I says that to myself as soon as I hear about your mare dying. 'Pat'll want a horse,' I said; 'something that'll work'."

"H'm," says Pat, only slightly touched by Mr Hicken's solicitude.

"Mind you," continues Mr Hicken, almost tearfully, "it isn't that I don't want to part with Dolly — I do. She's a bit fast for me. I said, 'I'll tell Pat she's fast, and if he doesn't want her, then he needn't take her. If he can't manage her, then that's his business, and he's only got to tell me'." Mr Hicken's eyes peer into distance, and he mutters away to unseen listeners. "I'd never expect a man to take a horse he couldn't work," he explains. "No, that wouldn't be the thing." Here he is interrupted by Pat Reggin, with caution in his voice.

"Well, I won't say I don't want a horse, Harry," he admits.

"No?"

"I do," says Pat in mild triumph, "but then it's got to be good, and at a fair price."

"Well I knowed that," says Mr Hicken eagerly. "I says 'Pat don't want a dear horse, and you can't ask a lot for a fast horse.' Now if my boy were home, he'd drive Dolly easily, but he isn't, and she's only eating her head off."

"I'll give her a go," says Pat, a little grandly.

"Ah," says Mr Hicken. He waggles a cautioning finger at Pat. "Don't tell me I didn't say she was fast."

"I'll put her in the slide," says Pat. "Double harness. You put the winkers on Baldy, Jim."

Baldy takes the newcomer quite naturally, submits harness, and stands quietly. "Stand here, Dolly," commands Mr Hicken. He fusses around her. "Here, you old tiger, get out of the way," says Pat.

"She's fast," says Mr Hicken.

"She'll stand," says Jim. "Let me get at her, Mr Hicken."

"Fast, you'd never believe it," says Mr Hicken.

"Don't tie her back, Jim," says Pat. "Give her a bit of trace, and a long coupling."

"She's terrible jittery when you go to hook her to the traces," says Mr Hicken with a worried expression.

Dolly stands calmly whilst the traces are hooked. This appears to surprise Mr Hicken no end so that he can only say "Goodness gracious me. Well, what do you know about that, eh? She never moved. Well, well." Then he adds, almost severely, "But she's fast, though."

Pat, who is a large man, red of flesh and face, white-haired, and commanding in the grand old manner, and more so, perhaps, in his farm clothes, stands astride the slide like a warrior at that. Jim, as befits the son of a warrior, walks behind.

No procession ever advanced more steadily. Sedately the slide moves forward, Dolly straining at the traces, prancing slightly, but undisturbed.

"Well," says Mr Hicken, puzzled and gratified, "thought she'd be faster." He keeps up with Jim, his legs wobbling in the effort. "Mind you," he gasps to him, "I had her in single harness."

"She's going well," says Jim.

"Well," agrees Mr Hicken admiringly.

"Wee-woa," says Pat. The slide draws to a halt. Dolly, with Baldy, stands quietly.

"Ruddy fine mare," says Pat, forgetting his buyer's manners in his affection for a good mare.

"Not too bad," says Mr Hicken eagerly. "I told myself that you'd like it. 'Pat can look after the fast ones,' I said."

"She might be fast," says Pat doubtfully. "I'll only give her the slide today, and perhaps this afternoon the bull-harrows. She can take the plough tomorrow."

"You won't know till tomorrow, eh?" says Mr Hicken with disappointment.

"I'd like to have her for a week," says Pat conditionally.

"Oh, yes. Oh, yes," says Mr Hicken. He ruminates. "A week, eh?" He looks at his neighbour. "Now to tell the truth, Pat, I was thinking about a couple of nice young heifers Jim

Andrews has over there. I was thinking if you liked the mare, then I could get them young heifers. If my boy was home, he'd say, 'Keep the mare,' but what good is it to me, fast and all that?''

"I'll tell you what," says Pat. "I've got a nice line of young Jersey stuff here. Springers too."

"Ah," says Mr Hicken, wagging a finger at his neighbour. "Jerseys, Pat. Jerseys. It's the reds I'm after."

"Blasted Shorthorns," says Mr Reggin.

Mr Hicken thinks, too, of the money in his hand, and it is a great enjoyment for him to feel the money, or to stare at a cheque. The rarity of occasions when he is able to fondle money has greatly increased his liking for the experience.

"Well, if you want to, try her for a week, Pat," he says reluctantly.

"That mare's all right," says Pat suddenly.

"You haven't tried her," says Mr Hicken shrilly. "She might jib. She mightn't work. And," he says, in a last desperate attempt to convince, "she's fast."

"Fast me ruddy old Aunt Maria," says Pat. "She's not fast, Harry. Now what's she worth to you?"

"Fast and all?" insists Mr Hicken. "I'd have to take something off for that. I could never charge twenty quid for a fast mare."

"Nor for a slow one, neither," says Pat. "I'll give you fifteen, no more."

"Will you now?" says Mr Hicken eagerly. "Well, I never. I never thought Dolly'd fetch fifteen quid. She's terrible fast."

"Get my cheque-book, Jim," says Mr Reggin. "I'll write a cheque now for Harry."

Weakened, Mr Hicken makes a last attempt. "Now perhaps you'd better wait a day or two, eh, Pat?" he suggests.

Mr Reggin writes out the cheque, crosses it, and hands it to Mr Hicken. Mr Hicken is not at all loth to take it, but slight worry shows on his face.

Pat Reggin suddenly roars. "Now then, Harry, don't you tell me she's fast," he says with heartiness. "That mare's all right."

To prove it he takes the reins, flicks them ever so gently, and "ch-cks" to the pair, so that they move forward, over the grass. Pat turns and shouts that he'll return the harness in a few days.

"Ah, yes," says Mr Hicken mildly, but more to himself than Pat, so absorbed he is in his cheque. He gazes absently at it, recollects where he is, stares after the pair, and by this time Dolly has gathered herself into a slight trot. A little worried, Mr Hicken gazes at her, clucks, shakes his head, clucks again, appears set on telling Pat about the mare being a bit fast, perhaps, but finally shakes his head again and walks down the drive to the cyclone gate, fondling the cheque.

PRIVATE
AMNIG, V.C.

Aaron, a man of many years, is also a man of many children, and that is why, perhaps, he drowses this summer morning, nodding over his emery wheel in the small backyard of the siding cottage.

Any moment now Aaron may wake slowly to life, either to answer a yell to open the gate or to make certain that, if a train approaches, the siding gate is closed. Afterwards he will subside again, muttering to himself and drowsing as before.

If Aaron is a little tired, then it is not to be wondered at, for a man who has reared eighteen children is apt to be weary and not expected to be agile, and generally Aaron is unable to snatch a great deal of sleep during the day, because of the children who tumble about the cottage and the small backyard. This morning, however, it seems the heat has sent all Wirril Creek into a gentle torpor, a warm lazy daze which stills the hand of Aaron and commits him to restfulness over his bench of mechanical appliances.

Come evening and the cool creeping down from the foothills, and Aaron will be awake, his emery wheel spitting a splurge of bright sparks; and Aaron will bend over it like a bow, sharpening this tool or that, making a nicety of a blunted chisel or chipped plane blade.

What Aaron thinks from time to time is difficult to say, for Aaron, at any time, seems a little dazed. How easy, then, to put it to the account of his many children, but such a jibe is cheap and too facile. Aaron, in his own way, is proud of his tribe, and will not countenance joking in the matter. Only once has he been known to ask for assistance, and that was in the matter of his income-tax returns, when he was reassured by Mr Armstrong, the local postmaster, that he owed the Government nothing.

"In fact," Mr Armstrong told him, "I'm sure the Government must owe you something."

Aaron's gnarled hand, on this warm morning, droops over the still wheel. His eyes are half closed, his lips parted as he breathes heavily and slowly.

He does not hear the same Mr Armstrong as he walks tappingly down the road, neatly happy and trim from his Post Office Store.

"Mr Amnig! Mr Amnig!" calls Armstrong, his voice high with excitement. "Mr Amnig!" The excitement mounts to a point of falsetto.

Aaron wakes into life, brushing his thick hand across his lined face. He stares somewhat stupidly at the wheel before him, seeing it in some queer mysterious way as a symbol, a habit man has when he awakes, and then more consciously he hears the postmaster's voice.

"One minute. One minute," he grumbles, "I'll open 'em for you."

"Not the gates. Not the gates," says Armstrong with all excitement. "It isn't the gates today, Mr Amnig."

"It isn't the gates today." That phrase runs over and over in Aaron's mind. Another symbol perhaps. "It isn't the gates today." Well, then, what is it if it isn't the gates?

"It's a telegram," says Armstrong, and his clean slim fingers have it held at both sides, stretched out, the news written plainly for the eyes of the world to read. Aaron stares down at the telegram a trifle suspiciously, perhaps, but mainly wonderingly.

Armstrong stares down at it, too. His eyelids quiver somewhat, his blue eyes clear and keen, whilst his lips keep moving as though they would voice a great piece of news.

"He's got the V.C."

"Eh?" says Aaron. He peers up at Armstrong, puzzled. He

feels he might be asleep himself, and this postmaster a partly unwelcome figure in his dream. There is something too energetic about the dapper and tensed form of the messenger.

"The V.C.?"

"Yes, the V.C. Harold's got it for bravery."

"Ah," says Aaron slowly. This he can understand, although what Harold has ever wanted with bravery he does not quite know.

"The V.C., that's the Victoria Cross, isn't it?"

"It certainly is," says the young postmaster, "the finest decoration a man can have." Armstrong himself takes a pace down the road, some sort of an imaginary Victoria Cross swinging from his white silk shirt.

"The best a man can have," he says.

Aaron says nothing. He stands in the sun, pondering the slip of paper, the words of the postmaster and the son who has won this award. It all seems so much of a jumble to him, that he would prefer to be sleeping, or at least drowsing again, in the sanctuary of his workshop.

"Missus'll be pleased to hear it, I'm sure," he says.

"Of course she will," says Armstrong. He sweeps energetically around on one heel, his arms swinging towards the low blue hills. "We will all be proud to hear it, Mr Amnig." He says earnestly, "I'm proud to have known Harold."

"H'm."

Aaron wants Armstrong to take himself away. After that he will tell Harold's mother and that will be that. The young man, however, does not wish to go. He savours the vastness of his news and would advise Aaron concerning his new-found fame.

"To be the father of a V.C.!" He is still thinking in exclamations.

"H'm," says Aaron again after a time. He moves from one foot to another. Apparently mild, Aaron is inwardly a man with strong feelings, but the gift of expressing them has been denied him. He says, then, plainly, "Well, I'll tell the missus."

He has committed himself to going to the house, and moves towards it. The young man stares after him, and Aaron, shuffling, holds the piece of limp paper. At the house, however, a faint surge of excitement goes through him, and this irritates him. His voice shrills a trifle as he calls impatiently, ''Mum! Mum! Where are you?''

Mrs Aaron, when she appears, is certainly not prepared for such news. She has been dozing on the sun-swept verandah, facing the railway, and perspiration beads her flushed face. She blinks at Aaron and then says, ''Well, what is it now?''

''Here.'' He hands her the paper. She stares at it and then hands it back to him. ''What does it all mean?'' she asks.

Aaron takes the telegram from her, peers at it, turns it over and says, finally, ''Young Harold's gone and got a Victoria Cross.''

''Well, now,'' says Mrs Aaron. She cannot, for a moment, believe that, but after a second's thought she realises she knew it all the time.

''If ever anyone was going to get the Victoria Cross it was our Harold,'' she says triumphantly.

''Don't take no notice of that Armstrong feller,'' Aaron warns her. ''He's still standing up there on the road.''

''They'll make him a corporal now,'' says Mrs Aaron happily.

Aaron shakes his head. ''I don't think they'll do that — not now that the war's over.''

''Then,'' demands Mrs Aaron with triumph, ''how can he get the Victoria Cross if the war's over?''

''I don't know about that,'' says Aaron. He pauses a moment. ''I don't care, either.'' He turns and stumps up the yard towards his emery wheel and bench and the coolness of the workshop. Armstrong, watching him, walks away with a certain degree of disappointment registering on his face.

CONCERNING
GRASS

The two men, the tall one and the shorter, thin one, rode their horses up to Denny's front gate. It was dark, and Denny was almost asleep, but not quite. He heard their horses' hooves on the gravel, even through the heavy rain, and he lay still a moment, hoping they would pass.

"Hoi there. Anyone home?" came the shout.

"Anyone in?" said a lesser voice.

Denny did not curse. He just got up, struggled into a pair of trousers, and slipped a shirt over his shoulders. He lit the lamp and went to the door. Pushing it open a little he peered towards the gate, but could see nothing, because of the rain.

"Hullo there!" he said.

"Wet weather, eh?" shouted the louder voice.

Denny knew that, knew too that he would have to go to the gate. He put boots on, and an oilskin. He protected the lamp in the half-open fold of his coat.

The man with the loud voice was large on his horse, although his horse, restless and shifting in the lamplight, was large enough. The thin man, somewhat shorter by looks, was on a small bright-eyed mare. Both loomed towards him as the lamp swayed and changed focus of light. The rain shot towards Denny in silver slivers.

He peered up at them. The tall man leaned down over his horse. "Sorry to get y'out," he said.

"That's all right," said Denny.

"Want a paddock," shouted the man, as though Denny might not hear him.

"A paddock," said Denny, thoughtfully. He had been asked for paddocks.

"Thought you might have grass to give away," said the big man eagerly.

"It's good grass," the other man observed.

Denny agreed with that. "I was keeping it for my stock," he said.

The big man looked disappointed. It was then Denny heard the mob on the road, a dog yelping way back behind them, and all the time the milling on the gravel road, the low mooing and the confused movement.

"Got a mob out there, eh?" he said.

"She's some mob, too," said the big man. "Had to get them away from the river. The flood's terrible."

"It's real bad in there," Denny said.

"I would have lost the lot," the big man said. The other man beside him nodded; almost sleepily, Denny thought.

"I've got a small mob myself," he said to Denny.

"Three of us," shouted the big man. "We're all in the same boat." The word "boat" registered, associated itself with water and flood. "We need boats now," he said heartily.

Denny nodded. "I was going to get stock," he said slowly. "Wanted to pick up a few head and use it for myself. They're all asking for it."

"Only empty paddock along the road," said the big man, shaking his head.

Denny stood in the rain for the moment, considering. The cattle were edging nearer to them, and the smaller man shouted to his dog.

Denny looked up at them. "There's just the two of you, eh?" he asked.

The smaller man said, "Three of us. Another chap's back there. He's having a bit of difficulty with his mob. I was helping him, before."

The big man chuckled, and then roared at Denny. "House cows, they are. Every bloody one of them, house cows. He nearly has to pat 'em all. 'Get up, Juanita,' he says to one of them. 'Get up, Nora, I tell you, get along there.' " He chuckled again. "Every one of them house cows," he said.

The rain battered harder upon the trio. The cattle moved, shifting restlessly upon the road.

"You can have the paddock," Denny said, "but you'll have to put your mobs in together. There aren't any dividing fences."

"Both of us?" said the big man, eagerly. "Thanks a lot, mate."

"The three of you," said Denny, and the smaller man nodded. Denny could see now that he was harder in the face than the taller man, but seemingly quieter. He turned his mare, and threw an arm into the air.

"I'll tell Bill," he shouted as he went off.

"Bill'll be glad," said the tall man. "Him with his house cows."

He looked down at Denny. "You're doing us a good turn," he said. "Might have lost every head. Tried to keep them on those flats, but what can you do? The others had more sense and got theirs off before. We waited and now you can't get a paddock." He corrected himself, "Leastways we're lucky now," he said.

"There's good grass there," said Denny. "It hasn't been touched in months, and with all the rain."

The big man nodded, and leaned down, towards Denny. "I'll give you a good thing for it," he said.

Denny shook his head, negatively, slowly. "Share it with the other two, that's all," he said. "One and six will do me."

"I'll give you two bob," said the big man.

"Only one and six," said Denny, almost lazily.

"Of course," said the big man, "I'd wait until they got another paddock."

"Three of you, or none," Denny said.

The big man looked a trifle gloomy. Then he nodded, slapped his horse's neck, and shouted, for he heard the others coming, "One and six to the lot of us, then, and all in together." He was very hearty.

The man with the herd of house cows was short on his small stocky horse. He had no stockwhip in his hand, but a few twigs of wattle. He sat forward on his horse, and looked down eagerly at Denny. He was red in the face, and fat too, with a slouched hat placed squarely on his hair. The rest of his face was fat, humping up, almost into folds, as he sat.

''Glad! Lord I was glad when they told me. Grass! You just can't get it, and the stock pinched and miserable.''

''They'll fatten on that,'' Denny said, ''if they'll fatten anywhere.''

''Thank the Lord,'' breathed the short fat man. ''That's the end of our troubles.''

''Well, come on,'' said the big man. ''We'll put 'em in.''

''Say you put yours in first,'' the fat man said to him, as though he were at a picnic. ''Then Harry can put his in, and I'll put mine in last.''

''Least yours will stand in the rain,'' yelled the big man. He plunged his horse upwards in the light of the lamp. Then he cracked his whip, rather magnificently, and went towards his stock. Harry nodded, wheeled his horse and went after the big man. As he raced away he whistled his dog. The short fat man sat up straight, looked at Denny, and said, ''I'd better help them, perhaps.''

He went off, jogging, and Denny could see his hand bouncing up and down, and all the time clutching the twigs of wattle.

Denny waited until the cattle came along the road. Then he fastened the gate behind him, and walked along the fence to the paddock rails. He slipped them, and pointed, his hand black against the lamp. ''Straight in with the lot,'' he yelled, to be heard above the mob.

The big man nodded, pinched in his lips, and cracked his whip. It made a great to-do in the night, and then the mob shot forwards, their front legs outwards, planted against the mud as though they were being driven, unwilling, from behind. Their long upturned horns flashed whitely in the light, their eyes glared, and they snuffled the slime from their gleaming nostrils. He had a confused picture of baldy-faced steers with hair curling about the horns.

''Hoop there!'' yelled the big man. ''In there, you beggars.''

102

Harry edged the leaders towards the rails. They went through, suddenly, and the mob surged forwards, milled as it overflowed about the opening, and then was into the paddock, a rumble of hooves, a protest of bellows and lowing.

"Fifty head there," shouted the big man. "Fat they were, before the flood."

They had seemed pinched up, cold and tired, to Denny. He watched them tucking into the grass.

"Now yours, Harry," said the big man. He was still staring towards his stock.

Harry and the big man turned back on to the road, and cantered away. When they came back they were droving steers, black steers which might have been nuggety and heavy on good grass, with no cold rain. Now they were miserable, in-drawn and humped. Harry cracked his whip, moving amongst them, touching one here and there with the butt of his whip. "Come along, come along," he kept saying.

The big man cracked his whip, time and time again, but for all that the small stock took their time. Harry stood at the rails, counting them. When he finished he began coughing, steadily, as though he were used to coughing, and not at all worried about it.

"You go inside," Denny said. "I'll help the other chap with his."

"Bill?" said Harry, cheerfully enough. "No, I'll help Bill. His stuff will come when he calls them." He grinned, and cocked a suggesting finger towards the big man. "Horace here gets real wild about Bill and his cows, but Bill's in love with his stock, and Horace can't see that." He coughed and said, "Not that Horace isn't, either, but in a different way."

When they brought Bill's stock along it was at a slow pace. Denny waved the lamp, lazily, up and down, backwards and forwards, and all the time the rain beat down, prinking the long sheeted water on the road. The warm glow in the centre of the lamp reproduced in the small drops on Denny's fingers.

The cows were Jerseys, silver, some of them, and the rest dark, almost black. They seemed a trifle bewildered, but for all that they plodded steadily forwards, their heads nodding up and down, the frost white of the rain fringing their soaking dewlaps. Eyes, large and soft were turned towards Denny. He stopped waving the lamp, and they went past him, into the paddock.

In the rear was Bill, beating a recalcitrant beast with wattle twigs.

"You old nuisance," he kept saying, affectionately. "Dash you, you old nuisance."

Then they were all there, in the paddock. The big man sat on his horse, his arms folded, staring down at Bill. Bill counted and then nodded. "Forty-four," he said, "of the best."

The big man snorted. "They'll be dead in the morning," he said, "if my stock gets near them."

Bill seemed not to have heard him. "They'll last anything out," he said, "now that they've got that grass."

"You know," he said to Denny, "it's surprising what Jerseys'll go through. Some people won't have that, but I know it." He seemed settled now, ready and eager to talk all night.

The night had nearly gone, because the light of Denny's lamp seemed almost ineffective. There was a luminous glow around the whole skyline, as though the rain in itself contained light, and was spreading it outwards. It was a faint sheen, white, almost to silver.

"It's nearly dawn," said the big man.

"We've had that stock going all night," said Harry.

"Mine since four yesterday," said the big man. "I'm further back than the rest."

"You should see it," Harry said to Denny. "People pulling their trucks through the mud with other trucks, and mud everywhere, and dead cows, and stock. There isn't a bite for any beast."

The big man shivered at the thought of it. "Gaw'struth, it's terrible. I lost ten head before I got out. Saw my baldy bull go down the river, and not a thing I could do."

"That's jolly rotten luck," Bill said. "It hurts to see that."

The big man nodded.

"Hungry!" Harry said, commencing to be talkative. "There wasn't a thing to eat, so Bill and me thought we'd have a chook. 'What's a chook, here and there?' I said to Bill, 'when everyone's not worrying about their birds, but only about stock.' Bill thought we shouldn't, but I thought we should.''

''I was only thinking about my own fowls,'' said Bill, ''but they went into the river, all except the rooster, that is. He stood on the bank, with the water swirling near his toes, looking at the hens and wondering what it was all about. He couldn't make it out at all.''

''But we're safe now,'' the big man said happily. He sighed and stared across the paddock. The stock was knee high in grass, which by daylight was green to be seen. It must have appeared something of a dream to them, Denny thought.

''You'll find the creek, all right,'' he told them. ''Just down the hill there, and no boggy spots.''

The three men nodded. Light came greyly over the paddocks, and the four men could see stock grazing. Although the rain was beating heavily the stock held against it.

''Well, there's no point staying longer,'' the big man said. He stared at Harry. ''Coming, mate?'' he asked.

Harry said he wasn't. Bill was looking at the cow which had lain down in the grass. ''Old Jenny, eh?'' he said, half to himself, as though he had thought this might happen, all the time. ''So she's calving, eh?''

The big man didn't even look interested. He nodded to Denny before he brought his horse past the rails. ''I'll fix up later with a cheque, Mr, Mr . . .''

''Simmons,'' said Denny.

''Simmons. Good. Well I'll fix you up during the week. One-and-six we said, eh?''

He waited until Denny nodded, and then he went off, flourishing his whip as though it still counted. He sped up the road, and the horse spurted water sideways.

''He'd have given two bob last night, or four bob, for that matter,'' said Harry, ''and now he's got his horse galloping.''

''I'll take a look at that cow,'' Bill said. ''She came in difficult last time.'' He went across to the cow, and it stared up at him as it writhed and strained.

Denny and Harry looked at Bill helping the cow, and they nodded, each understanding.

"Do that big bloke good to rear Jerseys, especially from poddies," said Harry.

They watched the light strengthen and lengthen, and Harry said suddenly, "I was telling you about the chooks we killed. Hell, we were hungry. We caught two of them in the corn, or Bill did really, and we had to wade to them waist-high. He was pretty quick catching them, considering his build. They flapped and squawked, but we pretty soon plucked them. We only had salt, so we had to boil them, and they didn't smell the best, but no chook smells much when it's plucked and lying there stone-cold naked. They didn't smell so bad when we had them boiling, and our tongues were nearly hanging out, for what with keeping an eye on stock, and pulling them out of water, we were pretty famished. All the time they were cooking Bill kept on saying, 'Do you think we ought to have done it?' but by the time they were cooked he thought so."

Harry grinned. "When we went to eat them they were stinking. Couldn't touch a mouthful of them. They'd been eating the green grubs in the corn, and stank when you put your nose near them."

He shook his head, a trifle ruefully. "I wanted to eat that chook, too. I kept remembering Mersing in Malaya during the show there, and the chooks we had got from a boong's place, seven hens and one rooster. We ate them on Christmas Day, with white sheets for tablecloths. Tokyo warned us they were going to bomb us out that day, but they didn't. We had seven hens and a rooster between six. They were good."

He began coughing. Denny listened to him, somewhat anxiously. "You'd better come inside with me," he said. "You can get warm, and dry those clothes."

"I'll give Bill a hand," Harry said. "That cow's going to have difficulty."

Denny looked at Bill, and then at Harry, now shivering. "Bill'll be all right," he said. "He knows cows."

"Oh yes, he knows cows all right," said Harry.

"Come on then," Denny said. Nevertheless, before they went to the house they both watched Bill, kneeling there, beside his cow. He was talking to it, as it stared up at him with half-wild eyes, and all the time his hands were pressed against its heaving sides, and at last he bent down, saying some words, and he began to take hold of the partly-born calf, pulling it, gently, and all the time crooning his words, whilst his eyes were soft as those of a mother itself, or a calf, for that matter.

THE
LITTLE
OAK

"Eff you go, you go," said Mr Weidel.

That was obvious enough, both to Claude and Mr Weidel.

"Eff you don't go, you don't go," Mr Weidel said, and this time he shook his head, to and fro, backwards and forwards. "She is vairy wet," he said mournfully.

He looked at Claude, seated on his dray and pondering. He looked at the nuggety chestnut draught, the thick competent wheels of the vehicle, and lastly at the milk-cans mounted on the dray behind Claude. Mr Weidel loved his milk-cans, as indeed he loved all things Weidel. Mr Weidel's love for his possessions was like the grey torrent which moved past him, powerful and undeniable, and his love for his milk-cans was no less than, say, his love for his cows or his wife.

And the milk; that was why he wished Claude to know before he urged the chestnut forward, that his, Ernie Weidel's, cans were aboard.

"Hooh!" he said suddenly. "What if she go, hey? What you do then, Claude?"

Claude was either not committing himself, or was his usual self, seemingly thoughtful, but really only dull. "That oak," he said suddenly, turning to Mr Weidel. "That's the old oak."

"Ha!" said Mr Weidel, easily able to keep up with Claude's thought-processes.

"So if she's only up to there," said Claude triumphantly, staring at the flooded stream.

"But she ain't," said Mr Weidel, alarmed. "She ain't only up to there."

Claude looked at his neighbour with astonishment, dignified

astonishment too. "If she's up to there, she's up to there," he said ponderously, unremittingly.

"Eff she iss, she iss," said Mr Weidel, lapsing in his enunciation because of his despair. "And," he added, "eff she issn't, she issn't."

"But she is," said Claude, now a trifle bewildered. "Safe she is at that point." He clung to this thought grimly, apprehensive of Mr Weidel's violent denials.

"She is not the oak," said Mr Weidel, breathing heavily.

Claude shook his head. He did not have to ponder the matter. He knew.

"Reckon she is," he said, trying to convince his neighbour. "Dad says she's all right if she's only up to the little oak."

"Ah," said Mr Weidel with sorrow and apprehension. "She iss not the liddle oak but the big oak."

Ten years of living in the valley had made Mr Weidel much like his neighbours, but there were minor differences, such as his habit of housing stock in the winter, and bedding them on cut bracken, and then carting to his cultivation the mess of bedding and manure. He himself had almost forgotten he was a foreigner. Now the differences were beginning to break down, and all because of Claude's stupidity.

"Just a reffo," said Claude to himself, as though that explained all.

"Silly he iss," said Mr Weidel under his breath.

"Giddup," Claude told the chestnut. "Eff you do" — Mr Weidel warned, still under his breath.

It was not that Claude wanted to go across the river. Oh, no; and not in this weather, either, with the grey skies threatening to break again and swell further the already high river. Even if it was only up to the little oak, yet its current could be strong. And Claude could not swim. Claude knew he could not swim. On the other hand he was not prepared to allow Ernie Weidel to drive the chestnut across, for he knew, in a vague sort of way, that it was wrong to let a foreigner think he could do what you couldn't. Besides, they would laugh at home, and never allow him to forget the occasion.

"Giddup, Bonny," he said, and Bonny moved. But she didn't seem to like the situation. She turned her head sadly and gazed upstream, turned it again, and gazed wistfully downstream. She stood, the water lapping her fore-hooves whilst she waited a further command.

"Giddup, Bonny," said Claude, almost fearfully this time. Great moving sheets of water always filled him with a nameless terror, a feeling strange to one who feared neither man nor farm beast, but only ridicule.

"Ah, you better come back," said Mr Weidel gently.

That part of Mr Weidel which loved his cans, and that other part of him which loved humanity — even such dull-witted humanity as Claude — fought a great battle. Not to have his milk sent was a great sorrow to the Swiss. To lose it in the river a terrible thing. Yet not even Mr Weidel thought his cans would go down the river.

When Bonny heard that last fearful "Giddup" she knew quite well that all was over with her, and yet out of sheer habit she stepped into the stream. The cold water slipped up to her fetlocks, then suddenly to her very belly. Bonny flayed her legs wildly, and the cart moved into midstream.

"Hey," shouted Claude. "Whoa-back there, Bonny."

Mr Weidel clasped his huge fists together, tensed his tremendous forearms and raised them above his head. "Ho, Claude," he said, shocked.

Bonny knew nothing about Mr Weidel's despair, or Claude's terror, or any command he might have given her. She struck out for the farther bank, plunging against the ceaseless roar of the downflowing river. Claude felt suddenly horrified, abruptly aware that life was intensely alive, that it had lost its old steady tempo, and was now beating up against him with fearful ferocity. "Bonny!" he shouted. "Come back, Bonny!" and when Bonny would not take notice he pulled frantically on the reins.

"Oh, no, Claude," shouted Mr Weidel. He stood on the bank and danced. "Oh, no Claudey," he cried. "Do not do that pleess!"

Claude, like Bonny, could hear no voices, and by now could see no animal, not even Mr Weidel, and the cart beneath him was moving convulsively, something like an unbroken colt on trial. Then Claude, still clinging desperately to the reins, found himself being swept downstream.

Mr Weidel shrieked in despair. He could see his cans tumbled into the water, and the horse struggling in the entrapping shafts, trying to free itself. Mr Weidel's coat came off, his old and shiny vest, his sweater which had been green and white, his collarless shirt, his bracered trousers, his undervest. His long woolly underpants, too, and his farm boots. Then in plunged Mr Weidel.

In that tearing river Mr Weidel was not dismayed. His tremendous arms fought back the rapid current, and his body refused to be swept downstream like panicky old Bonny and terrified Claude. Not a word, not a gasp, but, with his powerful arms cleaving the water, Mr Weidel edged across the stream to Claude, who was beating the water, flailing in terrified manner with his arms, and shrieking too, taking in lungfuls of river.

''Now,'' said Mr Weidel triumphantly. He put a hand out to Claude, and Claude, his eyes horrified, grasped it and clung.

''Not so high she iss, hey?'' said Mr Weidel. ''If you can stand, hey?''

But Claude was not standing. He was clinging to Mr Weidel, his breath coming in gasps, his eyes staring wildly, his whole being anxious to impart to his rescuer the fright which was his own. Claude, and the raging stream — the latter higher than both had thought — were almost too much for Mr Weidel. ''Hey, no! Hey, no!'' he kept telling Claude, and then when the young man struggled, his maddened activity almost drawing the farmer under, Mr Weidel swung his fist and clouted Claude across the face. ''And that,'' he added, hitting again.

Claude might not have noticed, or perhaps it served to increase his own terror. He continued clutching to Mr Weidel, perhaps trying to draw him under, trying in fact to climb on top of the Swiss and so escape the horror of that grey moving water.

Then whilst Bonny and the empty cart were swept downstream, the rain came beating across the water, darkening the afternoon, blotting out the banks.

Mr Weidel, at all times prepared to speak rapidly and give advice, now kept his words to himself. He struggled grimly with his neighbour's son. He forgot, even, about his milk and the cans, and purposefully set himself to overpower the frantic youth. It was not that Mr Weidel knew much about lifesaving, either, but instinct told him that Claude must be quietened. Mr Weidel raised a clenched fist and brought it down upon Claude's broad head. Claude still continued to struggle, and the more he struggled the more Mr Weidel thumped at the broad thick skull.

The rain had cleared before Mr Weidel, exhausted, succeeded in reaching the bank from which he had started. He might have collapsed into the river, on the very edge of it, and have dropped Claude had it not been for Claude's father, and his other neighbour, Lennie Conlon. They both moved into the water, grasped Claude and Mr Weidel and pulled them clear.

"Thought it'd happen. Thought it'd happen," Lennie Conlon kept saying.

"Ah, yes," agreed Mr Weidel in an exhausted voice.

"Can't go in water up to there," Lennie said severely, shaking his head.

"Good on you, Ernie," Claude's father said. He was white as his son, breathing heavily.

"Ah, don't talk about it," said Mr Weidel, still gasping. He began wiping the water from his limbs. Lennie drew off his coat. "Use this," he said.

"Me?" said Mr Weidel. "I am wet. My clothes are also wet. I shall put them on and go home."

"Never should've tried it," Lennie was saying.

Claude was lying white and still, no movement in his body and limbs.

"Perhaps the doctor, eh?" said Mr Weidel, putting on his undervest.

"You're right," said Claude's father with a frown. "But you'd better go, Ernie. You'll catch death of cold."

Mr Weidel peered down, pulled back Claude's eyelid and stared. "O.K.," he announced triumphantly. "But better be made warm, eh?"

Lennie and Mr Waddell stopped to pick up the great weight which was Claude. Mr Weidel finished putting on his sweater and coat, after which he followed them, carrying his own boots.

Then a fearful thought came to him. "The milk," he said.

"Forget about it," Lennie said. "We shouldn't't've tried it."

"But the cans," said Mr Weidel, overcome with grief.

Claude's father half-turned to look at Mr Weidel. "Now just don't you go worrying about those cans, Ernie," he said confidently.

"No, eh?" said Mr Weidel, brightening visibly.

"In there half an hour you were, I reckon," Lennie said. "Saw you, we did, and whipped straight down."

"Just don't worry about those cans," said Mr Waddell. He shook his head and gasped a bit, for Claude was heavy. "Saved my boy, you did," he said. He gave Mr Weidel a reassuring look. Who would worry about cans at a time like this?

"I will help," said Mr Weidel, who was now recovered. With Lennie and Mr Waddell he gasped all the way to the farmhouse.

The papers, of course, made quite a thing of it, and it did serve to show how high the river could rise in flood time. But not only the papers. The wireless, too, and the entire valley savoured the morsel of news which concerned them directly. Claude, listening, shook his head in dull wonder. Mrs Waddell clucked, and Mr Waddell looked severely at his son.

"Might 'a' got drowned, Claude," he said reprovingly. "Might easily 'a' got drowned."

Mrs Weidel looked at her husband with new interest. "That wass wonderful, Ernie," she breathed.

But Ernie was unimpressed. "It wass silly," he insisted. "All those cans." He paused. "And the milk," he said

113

sorrowfully. He remembered Mr Waddell and he brightened.

Early next morning he was down at the Waddell farmhouse. "The cans," he shouted into the gloom. "Have you found them, Mister Waddell?"

"Cans?" said Mr Waddell as he emerged from the dairy. "What cans?"

Then he remembered. "Ah, no, can't say we have. Got Bonny though, and she's all right, but the cart'll want two new shafts."

Mr Weidel followed his neighbour into the dairy and the lamplight. "But the cans?" he said fearfully.

"M'm," said Mr Waddell gloomily. "We haven't come across 'em yet."

It was not until he was back at his own dairy that the Swiss realised Mr Waddell had not been much interested in the Weidel cans. "No, but that cannot be," he kept telling himself. "He will find them, yess."

But Mr Waddell did not find them, nor Mr Weidel, although he walked up and down the river banks. When the torrent of water receded he waded downstream, inspecting every twist, every nook and cranny, every turn of the river. He felt under snags and in the shadow of dark rocks, but no milk-cans were to be found. He could see them in his mind's eye, turned and tossed by the water, rolled everlastingly until they reached the ocean itself.

Mr Weidel, to cover his gloom, might have gone into Brookvale and heard the fine things that were being said about him, by folk, and in the Brookvale *Register*, but instead he mooned about his farm, regretting his great loss, and waiting for his neighbour to come, and, perhaps, present him with some shiny new cans. He was not to know that people spoke about a medal, a citation, a presentation even, though the latter was even vaguer than the honours, and died a natural death because it somehow became associated with money and giving, and, strangely enough, the fact that Mr Weidel was, or had been, a foreigner, and was still a bit if it came to that.

But the idol of the day had only thoughts for his cans. He missed them. His can-racks seemed empty, and on the strength of it he decided to visit his reluctant neighbour.

He was well received until it came to the matter of cans. Then Mr Waddell sighed and said it had been a great loss for them all, the milk and the cans, especially the cans. He evaded his neighbour's eyes at this juncture, looked up at the ceiling, and brought the subject around, very adroitly, to Claude.

Mr Weidel's interest in Claude had waned, if, indeed, he had ever been much interested in that youth. He harped on the subject of cans. He even asked outrightly about replacements, but Mr Waddell seemed astounded, and even horrified, and in a fit of rage the Swiss bounced out of the Waddell kitchen and hurried home.

Next day he was back, and the day after until the Waddells became highly indignant at his repeated demands. "Who does he think he is?" Mr Waddell demanded.

It was on Mrs Waddell that the Swiss concentrated. Knowing something of a mother's love for her children, he reckoned his efforts might here bear fruit, but Mrs Waddell was a true farmer's wife. Losses were losses, come how they may, and one should be prepared to take them without demands of reparations or compensation.

"And," she told Mr Weidel indignantly, and thus shifting the responsibility, "you let my Claude take them across. What did you do that for, hey?"

"It wass not the liddle oak," protested Mr Weidel, weak with anger. "And I told him not the liddle oak."

Claude seemed to have forgotten the incident. Vehement though the Swiss's denunciation of his family were, Claude continued to pick up his neighbour's cans twice daily. He would stand patiently and listen to the sorrow and anger in the Swiss's voice. But never once did he thank the dairyman for having saved him. It were as though he accepted life as it came, hard continual toil, dances occasionally, even death visiting him and death repulsed, one was not surprised at any turn life might

115

take. And Ernie, castigating, would be almost reduced to tears. It was not to be believed, this obtuseness, this acceptance of everything that happened.

There was a great chuckle along the Valley and few expressions of disapproval when the Waddells sealed the incident by publicly announcing through the medium of a four-shilling notice in the Brookvale *Register* that they were grateful to those connected with the recent saving of their son Claude from drowning. This was considered a clever move, a triumph in strategy. Coincidental, of course, was the near-by advertisement of Rogers and Son, General Storekeepers, announcing the sale of new ten gallon milk-drums, non-spillage type.

But as Mr Weidel rarely read papers, he probably missed that gem. He did realise, however, that his chances of being compensated had faded. He did not miss the failure of the Governor-General to pin a medal upon his breast and read a fine citation. The press had forgotten him, being interested in foreign affairs and the major event of the coming annual show, so that Mr Weidel continued to mourn, on his hillside farm, the saddening duplicity of human nature.

And then, one evening, Claude, at the usual time, rumbled up to the dairy slightly excited, urging Bonny along at unusual pace. Instead of picking up his neighbour's cans he jumped from the cart and clanged to the concrete three ten-gallon cans.

Mr Weidel came running from his dairy. At first he thought they were his own cans, but on closer inspection he found them to be of a different type, the coveted non-spilling variety. No, they were not his own. He was sad.

And Claude beamed. Claude, whose smiles were rare. "There you are, Ernie," he said proudly. "That's to make up for the cans *he* never gave you." Claude gestured contemptuously towards his father's house.

"No!" said Ernie. This he could not believe. He continued to stare at the young neighbour.

"Got 'em at Brady's sale," Claude said proudly. "Got 'em

for almost nothing, I did.'' He stood there, pondering lovingly the cans he had bid for, feeling again the excitement of competing with experienced bidders. ''Mind you,'' he apologised, as though meaning it, ''they mightn't be as good . . .''

He got no further. ''Claude,'' shouted Mr Weidel. ''Oh, Claudey.'' He wanted to hug Claude, great oafish Claude, and knew that the young man would not like that, so in his excitement all he could do was run around the cans, patting them lovingly, lifting the lids, looking into them, replacing the lids and not noticing the few bumps here and there received in the course of their lifetimes.

After a time the grinning Claude pushed his hat to the back of his head, rubbed his forehead and reckoned he'd better be going. With that he lifted the full cans of milk on to his cart, assisted by the excited Mr Weidel. Then Claude took his farewell, occasionally glancing back with proud and loving looks at the three cans by the dairy door.

Ernie, for his part, was torn between the desire to look at the same cans and handle them and to wave to the dull boy who had restored his faith in humanity. But after a time he could no longer contain himself, and with a final wave to the driver of the rattling cart he dashed forward, seized a can and began running with it towards the house, shouting his glad news as he went and crying ''Mary! Mary! Come and see. Oh, Mary, the cans, the cans, the cans!''

GRANDMA
SELLS
PERSIMMONS

Grandma sells persimmons. She sits all day on the front
verandah, waiting for the buyers to come. Her hands are folded
on her lap, for she has long ago given up the silly idea of sewing.
"Nothing in it," she says.

There is nothing in anything it seems, other than selling
persimmons. She calmly takes the money when they give it to
her, nods, nods all the time until they are out of the gate, into
their car or utility. She watches them drive away, listens to
them change gears as they pull up the gradual slope of the hill,
and knows that in the spot where the tallowwood grows beside
the road they will pause, almost as though they were about to
turn around, come back to buy more persimmons. Here they
change gears, and Grandma nods to herself, opens her hands
and looks down at the threepences and other silver coins
nestling there.

Usually she is paid in threepences, as though people think
that if they rid themselves of a few spare threepences they are
not spending anything, really. Grandma then closes her hands
and waits for more buyers to come.

All sorts come. There are those, very keen, but just a little sly,
a trifle slick. They come from the city, and they think Grandma
will sell them persimmons, almost for nothing, like the cream
they want to buy from her and butter if she has it. When they
find they may only buy persimmons they decide they shall go
back to the city and say, "Persimmons? Persimmons? Why, I
know a place along the Coast Road where you can get them for

nothing. Next to nothing, anyway.''

They say, earnestly, ''You know, these country people don't know what they are giving away. Sixpence a dozen the old girl asks, and down here you pay one and sixpence a dozen. Look at that now! Penny ha'penny down here, ha'penny up there.'' They are very pleased about that.

Grandma sits on the front verandah, and looks at the yellow persimmons and then down at her hand with a few threepences in it. She has sold a dozen to the last car. Clever man that, by his own reckoning. Clever all right. He thought he was getting away cheaply. You could see it in his face, looking at the persimmons, calculating how much there was in just one tree, the tree from which he had picked his golden beauties. A man could make a bit, just out of that one tree. Grandma had sat on the verandah and watched. Finally he had only taken a dozen. Pity, he had thought, driving away, all that money going nowhere. Two threepences in Grandma's hand.

''If I had to box 'em,'' she thinks, ''buy the boxes, pack 'em, then hammer the lids down. Then get Jerry to take them in the service-car to the station. What would the boxes cost? What would nails cost, and Jerry taking them to the station — that is, if Jerry remembered to call and take them.''

Grandma looks down at the threepences and thinks about agent's fees; or agent's bills, for Perce Anderson got a bill back for his peas.

There are others who buy Grandma's persimmons. Some of them stop in rather nice cars, polished cars. No scratch on the paint, no mud on the mud-guards. Polished-looking men and women, but only polish Grandma is inclined to think. They want persimmons.

''Good gracious,'' says the man as he comes through the gate. ''We are in luck, that's if they'll sell. Persimmons! Haven't seen them for years. Didn't think you *could* get them.''

The polished man, who has his wife with him, says, ''I say, are your persimmons for sale?''

119

"They're for sale," says Grandma, looking straight at him.

"Then I'd like a dozen," says the man. He looks at his wife. "Perhaps we could even make it two dozen, eh?" He feels he is being benevolent towards both his wife and Grandma.

"Sixpence a dozen," says Grandma.

"Ah," says the man. He looks about for the fellow who is going to pick them for him, but there isn't any fellow. He looks a bit uncertain, but Grandma seems not to care whether he takes them or not so that eventually he walks over to the tree, a little self-consciously, and begins to pick persimmons, mainly from the lower branches. All the best fruit has been picked lower down, as he is not the first polished person to have stopped at Grandma's, and, polish and all, he looks for the best, sees them higher up, begins to reach to them, cannot, grasps a branch and hauls himself high.

Tie comes out of the vest, clothes a bit awry, but he forgets that in the fascinating search for the best. Nothing stops him; he is out, determinedly, for the best. The woman gives a smile to Grandma, and a queer look to her husband, whom she seems to see in a somewhat different light. He looks flushed about the face and wears a triumphant expression.

Sometimes the polished people have little polish. They are ever so polite to Grandma. They don't mind getting up the tree. They speak in polite distant voices, husband to his wife, wife to her husband, as though they really don't know each other, haven't known each other for a long time. Might be the first time they have met.

"Oh, I say, dear, do you really think we need a dozen? You know, we won't be into Sydney before Monday, and that is a long time to keep them."

"I don't know, dear," says her man as he climbs the tree, "that you can't keep the ones that aren't too ripe some considerable time perhaps."

"I'd be careful, dear," says his woman, watching him climb, "that you don't get your trousers caught in some of those branches."

"I am, dear," he says, meaning "careful", and not sounding too intimate.

"I have some hard ones, dear," he tells her.

"Let me see them," she says, and her man dutifully shows them. She looks at them with a stare as hard as the unripe fruit.

"Oh, dear, they will never ripen. You can't pick fruit like that, dear."

Well, he can but he won't. "Can't put them back on the tree, dear," he says. Grandma is watching them from the verandah, so he can't drop them.

He gazes a trifle sadly at the three he has picked, and finally throws them to his woman. After that he picks the yellowest, the most golden you might say, those with a touch of red on the curved tips. Then he gets quite enthusiastic, for although he has picked a dozen he sees a couple of beauties, further up, and he may not resist them. He throws them down.

"That's over the dozen, dear," she says.

Oh, they'll make it two dozen. They make it three. One and sixpence in Grandma's hand. No boxes, no nailing down the lids, no depending on Jerry to pick up the blessed cases. Anyway, how would Grandma pick them? Perhaps Grandpa might pick them.

Not Grandpa. He sits inside, for he likes a fire, even if autumn is yet young. He'll have nothing to do with persimmons. He curses those trees at night, when the flying-foxes swoop down from beneath the mountain, and commence their bickering and squabbling, keeping it up all night.

"Hullo, lidy," says the man who is out to do business. He might be a barrowman (on a holiday, of course). He has green corduroy trousers, his sleeves are rolled up and he wears bright tan shoes. "I see you have persimmons there, lidy," he says.

"Sixpence a dozen," says Grandma.

"Sixpence a dozen, now!" cries the barrowman, his eyes lighting up. But natural cunning makes him conceal his surprise.

"Tell you what, lidy," he says. "I'll take twenty dozen straight and give you fourpence a dozen."

"Sixpence a dozen," intones Grandma.

"But, lidy," he says, "I'm giving you an offer for twenty dozen. No risk on your part. The risk is mine. What might happen, eh? I might lose half of them through being overripe. Anything might happen. I take the risk. Now come on, lidy, I'll give you fourpence a dozen."

Grandma doesn't care if the whole lot goes bad on him. She don't care if he never makes a bean out of them. She doesn't even bother saying, "Sixpence a dozen," but just opens her hand, and the barrowman sees the silver threepences and sixpences in it, and he nods, gives a bit of a grin, forgets all he might lose, becomes hearty again.

"I'll take 'em," he shouts. "I'll take 'em if I lose the lot. Sixpence a dozen."

He takes them. Bert, his cobber, stands beneath the trees and catches all the barrowman throws to him. He puts them in a sugar-sack, two sugar-sacks, three sugar-sacks.

"How many's that, Bert?" he asks, and Bert says it must just be about enough, and they both give Grandma a look to see if she's been counting, and she is staring at them, so they think she must have been counting and they say, loudly, that they reckon it is enough, near enough, as though they might be leaving a few of their own, and the barrowman wipes his hands, finds money in a trouser pocket, and gives it to Grandma, a new ten-shilling note. Forty sixpences, eighty threepences. Grandma looks down at it, wonders a little, would rather eighty small coins.

The barrowman goes off through the gate saying he'll take the risk, lidy, dashed if he won't.

Grandma crushes the note in her hand. It has sharp little corners where it is folded, sharp like the man who gave it to her. Grandma smiles grimly. Never an end in the world to the people who think you are a fool.

A utility-truck creeps down from the north. It groans on the hills, creaks when it nears Grandma's, squeaks a little, staggers along carrying a burden of children and camping-gear. It sags past the persimmon orchard and hesitates. It groans and stops.

Children fling up a canvas tarpaulin, peer out. They see the persimmons.

"Look, Dad, persimmons!"

Dad crawls out from behind the driving wheel.

"I know," he says, a trifle irritated. That's why he stopped, he tells them. He'll see if they are for sale.

He feels in his pockets before he goes through the gate, as though he has made a fool of himself before, buying things and then not having the money; as though, too, he has often dreamt he has.

Grandma nods to him. She likes this sort of a sale. "Sixpence a dozen," she says as he raises his hat. The man nods, looks grateful, likes Grandma's voice, wanders a little, not knowing where to commence, what tree to choose. Finally he remembers and calls to the children, and they come tumbling across to him, through the fence, and up into the trees. He is bolstered up now by a handful of children, made a man by fatherhood.

"Now, don't break the limbs," he warns. He shouts an order to this one or that, and stands a trifle importantly, with his legs apart; but after a time he becomes a little anxious, for the family has deployed in different directions. Only Dick is up the tree above.

"Come down, Dick," he says quietly. He raises his voice to the others. "Come on, Rob, Betty, Allan. That's enough. We don't want to take the whole orchard."

"Neither you do," says Grandma, a trifle grimly. "You couldn't afford it."

Six dozen makes six sixpences. Five sixpences and a fumble for the other.

"Let the children have that dozen," says Grandma. "The ripe ones."

Well, they have them, anyway, their noses pushed into squashed fruit, golden fruit, broken fruit with juice orange-red, oozing. Some of them have found the date-plum persimmons, as dark as dates, and as sweet.

The man is going out the gate when he sees some yellow flowers. "Calendulas," he says, in surprise, turning to Grandma.

123

"Marigolds," says Grandma, nodding.

"English marigolds," the man says. "I'd like some seedlings if you have any to sell." He fidgets hurriedly in his pocket.

"Take what you want," says Grandma. "There's plenty of them under the old plants."

"For my heart," says the man. "The old ticker plays up a bit. Make a soup out of them, you know, and you can't beat it. Try to get the seedlings in town, can't get them."

He stoops down and scoops a handful of them from the soft wet soil. Grandma will not take a penny. She nods seriously when he repeats gratefully that they are for his heart.

She watches the utility stagger down the road, hears it lurch and groan, sees it sway, and finally disappear over the hill. She smiles then. Grandpa will snort when he hears that one — marigolds for the heart!

There is one more visitor for Grandma, one more at least. Another of those polished cars. The man who gets out of it is upright, overpolished. His wife is a stuck-up piece of goods if ever there was one, thinks Grandma, and although she is rarely moved by impulse, she thinks now that she would like to show these two a thing or two.

They come through her gate as though they don't want to, really, and wouldn't, actually, only that they want persimmons. The woman looks haughtily at Grandma and says, without a look at her husband, "How much are your persimmons?"

Grandma thinks she won't sell them at all, but then she thinks she will.

"Shilling a dozen," she says for the first time in her life of selling persimmons.

"A shilling seems a lot," sniffs the woman.

Grandma opens her hand, closes it. Ten shillings in that hand, two-shilling pieces, shillings, sixpences, threepences.

"We'll have a dozen, George," the woman says to her husband. She pays the shilling into Grandma's hand. The shilling is highly scented, like the woman.

124

She then waits to have the persimmons picked. She even gives a glance along the verandah to see where the man is who will pick them. Grandma's hand closes over the shilling firmly.

"Pick them yourself," she says. "Everyone does."

"I beg your pardon?" says the woman.

"They all pick them," says Grandma firmly. She holds the shilling tightly. "Don't expect me to," she says, even more firmly.

George picks them, but George does not want to. George takes the fruit from the lower branches. He will not be urged up trees. He hands each to his wife. Eleven persimmons. He holds one in his hand, stares at it, puzzled.

"What," he says to Grandma, holding up the persimmon, "is this?"

It is a persimmon with some dark muddy stain on it.

"Flying-foxes," says Grandma. She nods. "Vomit." The man stares at her. "They all vomit," says Grandma.

Click, they are gone, the gate shut, the polished car rolled away and dusk is rolling in. Grandma will soon go inside.

First she commences to count the coins. Threepences are herded in fours and sixpences in twos. Silver sheep. Heaps of threepences. There is a delight in fathoming the number of shillings in that handful of small coins. Down the road the clip-clop of a horse.

The horse is cantering now, pushing aside the silver-purple, the mist that lowers about the orchard, fumes gently along the rows of trees. Well, no one on horseback ever buys persimmons.

The horse is at the gate. It stops. The little halfcaste boy from the blacks' camp. Bad lot those blacks, Grandma thinks.

A wistful small face above the shaggy old bay. Looming large in the evening that bony bay. Two props for its front legs and the boy perched just behind the props, his large wistful eyes looking at the golden persimmons through the gloom. He does not see Grandma on the verandah.

"Want some persimmons?" shouts Grandma. She really

thinks you have to shout at dusk in order to be heard.

The halfcaste boy looks mildly scared. He is about to urge on his swaying horse, then thinks differently.

"Good evening," he says to Grandma in an ultra-polite voice.

"Good evening, yourself," she says.

The small fellow upon the horse makes a serious face. He speaks in a quaint manner, known as old-fashioned. "I would like some persimmons," he says, "but I haven't the money."

She knows he isn't trying to get a few for nothing. He is in earnest, the little fellow. Besides, he has interrupted her counting. Grandpa is inside beside the fire ready to snort. Plenty to tell Grandpa. Marigolds for the heart!

"Go on," she says abruptly. "Take some. Take as many as you like."

"Thank you," the small fellow says, with that Aboriginal lilt in his voice. "That's good of you."

"Fuh!" she snorts, and gets down to counting her sixpences, lining them up again in fours, piling them high. She takes no notice of him when he finishes picking his golden fill, his hoard that tumbles about him in pockets and shirt front, which slumps him a bit as he climbs on to the bay horse. Then he goes off in the gloom, and she wonders absently, as she gathers up the last of the coins, how the bay mare is able to carry such a load.

TALLYHO
THE
RED
RASCAL

The arm of coincidence, so often generous in actions for both writer and storyteller, was this morning doing a trifle of stretching for Mr Hicken, although that gentleman was quite unaware of anything other than that the morning was very fine. Mr Hicken, as he opened the gate of his fowlyard, was suddenly aware that the morning was very dismal indeed, and that the sun, if it insisted on shining, was brazen and unsympathetic.

For there, in and near the tall paspalum of his fowl-and-duckyard, lay the white feathers of Mr Hicken's fowls, and the plumage of Mr Hicken's ducks. Mr Hicken, who was usually fairly slow of reflex, became suddenly galvanised into alarmed sorrow. This increased as his gaze travelled and he beheld the gory corpses of ducks and fowls.

''Foxes!'' said Mr Hicken.

Mr Hicken, trembling with terror, scooped and felt the nearest bird. It was warm. ''Dead, too,'' thought Mr Hicken. His hairy fingers twitched about the limp bird. Heart beating, he bypassed a favourite Rhode Island Red, a heavy Orpington and a skinny Leghorn with legs stiffening towards heaven. He parted a clump of giant paspalum. It was then his agony was greatest, and a groan parted his lips.

''She ain't there!'' said Mr Hicken, and the truth was that she wasn't, neither Emma, his favourite duck, nor her twenty-five eggs, due, any day, to be hatched into the sweetest ducklings Mr Hicken and Emma had ever hatched. Mr Hicken, small tears in his eyes, stared with deadened sorrow at the empty nest and slowly but purposefully raised his head, his eyes and then, higher, a fist towards heaven, whilst he muttered that vengeance would be his lot, see if it wouldn't.

Another thought struck him, slowly, and he pondered it a moment, after which he searched about in the grass for a weapon. A half paling came to his searching fingers, and this he grasped, firmly, the light of battle gleaming in dimmed eyes. The warm fowl had made him believe that fox might still be within close radius.

He closed the fowlyard gate behind him, and then almost died of pure shock as he spied the fox, which, aflood with the brazen sun, was staring at him from a nearby bunch of bracken. It might not have seen him, so absent was its look, so preternaturally solemn its gaze.

''God bless us!'' said Mr Hicken.

The fox started a little at that, turned and ran a few yards. It then sat again and fixed another look upon the farmer. This sort of thing angered the owner of Emma, so that he swung his paling, whooped, and ran for the animal, which, even then, did not seem scared, apparently having some knowledge of Mr Hicken's age, weakness, and inability to run as fast as a fox. Nor was there a hound to sool on to this infamous beast, let alone a gun to shoot it. Mr Hicken almost burst with indignation over the whole matter. Long after the fox had gone did he talk to himself, in slow rumbles not customary to him, for he was, normally, a mild man.

He was still talking to himself, and deciding to have a yarn with old Tracey, when the long arm of coincidence elongated slightly, hovered about the Hicken establishment and came to rest on Mr Hicken, who, drooped over his front gate, was waiting for someone to share his indignation and fury.

By no stretch of the imagination could he be thought to resemble a fox, although, to be sure, his hair was reddish, ginger-red, harsh on his face and arms, and sprouting wildly over his head. However, it was not at the fellow Mr Hicken stared, but at the weird contraption which, horse-drawn, followed the stranger. It may have been an ordinary cart or dray, but the sounds it emitted were even more weird than its appearance, and as it came closer Mr Hicken could see that the sounds came from a bag-covered contraption. It barely smothered a strange and mournful wailing, an entire bedlam of sound which had a strongly depressing effect upon the already depressed Mr Hicken.

The fellow, when he drew abreast of Mr Hicken, betrayed a fine pride in his cart of wails. He even paused a moment or two to allow the wailing to have its full effect upon the watcher, and then, heartily, he said, "G'day."

Mr Hicken, who had a story to tell, said, more eagerly than upon other occasions, "Ha!"

"Nice day, eh?" said the man.

"No," said Mr Hicken deliberately. "Not very nice at all."

Far from depressing the stranger, this seemed to make his expression even brighter. "Oh!" he said.

"I've lost fowls today," said Mr Hicken bluntly. "And," he added, "ducks."

"Chooks," said the man rapidly. "Chooks, hey?" He approached Mr Hicken, his red beard bristling, his blue eyes fairly flaming. "You've lost chooks, mister!" He flicked a finger, raised his right hand in the air, and brought it down with alarming emphasis. "Do you know?" he said, peering into Mr Hicken's slightly excited face. "I'm going to tell you how you lost them chooks." He nodded, shook his head with violent emphasis, and said, almost hoarse in his whispering, "Foxes." He said no more, but drew back, as though, having uttered that one wild word, no more needed to be said.

"Yes," said Mr Hicken, awe-struck, and in similar tone. He did, however, recover quickly, not wishing to be done out of his unusual tale.

"Ten hens," he said, and as this appeared to astonish the man only slightly, he added, without blushing, "fifteen perhaps, with what they took away." The man nodded, as though it was understandable altogether. "And ..." announced Mr Hicken, no longer leaning upon the gate, but drawing himself to his full height and intaking his breath, preparing for the big announcement ...

" ... Duck and setting. Ducks and eggs," supplied the man calmly.

"Yes," said Mr Hicken, deflated, and suddenly helpless.

"Thought so," said the redheaded man.

He then disregarded Mr Hicken's floundering, and, at the same moment, whistled. Noise rose, weirdly, as the baying of hounds over the dark Styx, cries of the damned to be loosed, the mystery only being made clear when the red man uncovered the contraption in the cart to display a pack of foxhounds, baying and yelping, crying through the wire-netting behind which they were enclosed.

"Goodness gracious," said Mr Hicken. The sight startled him, rheuming his eyes slightly. "If only," he said to the stranger, "you had had them here this morning."

"It *is* this morning," the stranger informed him.

"Early," said Mr Hicken in explanation.

"Still get your foxes," said the owner of the hounds.

"Not now," said Mr Hicken sadly, from his accumulated bush-lore.

"Tallyho the red fox!" said the red man, suddenly grinning about some joke he knew. "Tallyho the rascal and we'll get him."

The words enchanted Mr Hicken. "Well, well," he said interestedly.

"Course we'll get him," said the man. "You watch."

He took one foxhound from the mass of tan and black drooping ears, and dropped him to the ground. The dog drew his body level with the earth, commencing from the moist tip of a nose until the tail only, at its tip, was above ground-level. Then he let out a wail and a squeak and a howl and a mournful note of joy, after which he stared at his master, awaiting orders. His master, pleased enough with this sort of exhibition, withheld that word to go.

"I'll let 'em all go?" he said to Mr Hicken.

"Oh, yes," said Mr Hicken eagerly.

As he fiddled with the cage-door the dogs set up a howling. However, when he opened it they did not attempt to emerge.

Then, with one mighty whoop, the red man ejected them. ''Tallyho the red rascal!'' he shouted at them, and a light came into their eyes and they escaped through the opening, dropping to the ground, their bodies following black noses which traced absurd patterns upon the ground. They were visibly excited, yelping, turning and twisting.

So, too, was Mr Hicken excited. He clasped and unclasped his hands, made nervous movements and wished the hounds would find the trail.

''Don't you worry, boss,'' the redheaded man said. ''They'll get him.''

''See that there bunch of trees near your creek?'' he told Mr Hicken. ''They'll find him there.''

''It isn't my creek,'' said Mr Hicken.

''That doesn't matter,'' said the man with slight disgust. ''They'll get him.''

Then, surely, they were running towards the creek and the clump of trees, weaving throughout the grass, never looking up, but howling and bursting into impatient noises until the leader let out a yell and fairly flew at the trees. Mr Hicken clasped his hands and thought of the fat fox, belly filled with Emma and her offspring. That fox wouldn't be able to run much. He saw the hounds tumble down the creek bank and become lost amongst the trees.

''Rushes there, eh?'' said the man. ''I'll bet there is.''

''Yes,'' said Mr Hicken tensely.

''Thought so,'' said the man triumphantly. ''Then he's there. Tallyho the red rascal, they'll get him.''

And so they might have. There was a shrill yelping, an excited high-pitched call and the next moment a brown bundle tossed itself through the air, bursting on the sight of the two men, becoming lost in the tall seeded grass. As it went it bounced and turned and twisted, leapt across ridges and flattened along undulations. It was lost and found, seen, lost and discovered, all in breathless moments.

On the hillside they played, the hounds and the fox, and the fox, cunning to the end, raced north, and then south, and, finally doubling on his own tracks, was lost again in the grove of trees. When Mr Hicken, trembling with fright and nearly dying from disappointment, thought the game lost, the fox came running, this time towards the very fowlyard it had last night raided, but close behind, their throats wide and baying their triumphant music to stir the blood of the old man, came the hounds.

The red man was stirred, too. "They'll get him," he muttered, and then, when the hounds might have missed their quarry, he rose to the tips of his toes and shouted loudly and long, "Tallyho the red rascal!" Mr Hicken thumped his thighs in incredible delight, shouted unintelligible words and whooped and screamed hoarsely until the fox itself was caught, captured and tossed into the air; and all the time the red man was laughing and shouting his war-cry.

"But of course, mister," said the man, "there is the matter of payment, hey?" He thrust his red bristles at the mild Mr Hicken.

"Payment," said Mr Hicken. His sorrow returned. He hated that word, or any like it. Payment, money, bills, they were all the shadows in Mr Hicken's life.

"A few juicy ducks, or a pair of hens, eh, what about that?" cried the man.

Mr Hicken relaxed slightly. "That's a lot," he said, and not without cunning, "for giving your dogs a feed of fox. I'll give you a hen."

"Two hens and a duck," shouted the hound-owner.

"Two hens and a duck," agreed Mr Hicken, with reluctance. Following Mr Hicken to the fowlyard, the stranger proceeded to eye the poultry. His knowledge of poultry was unimpeachable. None of your three-year-old loafers of laying fowls, no scaly legs for him, or even your second-year hens. He wanted pullets, just on the lay, and he selected two of the plumpest. The duck he chose caused a wringing of the heart to Mr Hicken. The dead birds, also, the redheaded man took, with assumed reluctance, telling Mr Hicken that he'd clean up that mess for him.

In rear of the dog cage was a smaller, bag-covered cage, and, the bags removed, a fine collection of birds was revealed, red and white and black and spangled varieties of fowls, none of them at all to be sneered at, and ducks also, and one goose, which had seemingly lost its honk. Into this cage were popped the two pullets and the duck.

''Now,'' said the red man, licking his lips and looking about triumphantly, as though to give Mr Hicken something for his money, or rather, his poultry. ''Now,'' he said, ''tallyho for the next red rascal!''

THE
INSPECTOR

Bertie Curtis was very thoughtful following the visit of the dairy-inspector. In his own quiet way he had secretly dreaded the coming of the official, and because he habitually prayed to God about the most intimate details of his day's work, he had often prayed about the inspector, petitioning God to give him at least some warning about that man's coming.

Take the bails for example; Bertie had promised himself that, being warned by God regarding the inspector's visit, he would immediately haul down, bag by bag, the ton of pollard and linseed meal stacked in the fourth bail. Then he would remove the feed-drums from the second bail, and the surplus of feed-sacks he was reserving for the wheat season when bags were at a premium. It would take some doing, but Bertie had promised himself he would manage it, even if it meant later restacking the feed in its rightful bail, the drums and feed-sacks in theirs.

But the inspector had come, with no warning except that his small roadster had pulled up outside, and he had uncurled himself from the driving seat, unfolded himself from behind the wheel. True, he had waited a moment to stretch, to reach his lank form towards the sky, after which he had advanced purposefully towards the Curtis house. Bertie, being a bachelor, had his house no tidier than the bails. To tell the truth Bertie had feed stacked in the house, too, his father's old room taking most of it, with the daily ration for the pigs in the storeroom, as well the pigs knew.

So it was Mr Kissop found Bertie, petrified almost, amongst his feed.

"Ah there, Mr Curtis," he said heartily, knowing for sure that he had the law on his side, and undoubtedly, on the other side, a lawbreaker. "Nice day, isn't it?"

"Lovely," Bertie told him earnestly. If Bertie had been able to roll his eyes they would have rolled with apprehension.

Ted Kissop rubbed his hands together. Long, capable hands they were, the hallmark of character, as Bertie acutely observed. "Just thought we'd pop down and look things over," said Mr Kissop, using a rather jovial royal plural.

"Ha," said Bertie, trying to enter into the inspector's delight. "Yes, of course, ha!"

"H'm," said Mr Kissop absently. He loved the trips around to the farms. He had a great respect for cow-cockies and their acumen, though rather less for their cleanliness. But what pleased him most was the sheer delight of travelling at the Government's expense, along endless stretches of road, turning into nooks and crannies of farm life, and being at no disadvantage, either.

"Things are a bit anyhow," said Bertie slowly. Then, with a rush, "What with the rain you know, and one thing and another."

"Ah, yes," said Mr Kissop kindly, as though this were the first time he had heard such a thing, and because of that it contained something interesting. "Certainly has been wet, Mr Curtis."

"Besides," Bertie told him eagerly, "I've just had twins."

Mr Kissop seemed to see nothing surprising in this, but he was delighted. "Different sexes, Mr Curtis?"

"Two heifers," said Bertie proudly.

"Fine," said Mr Kissop. "I can't remember many cases of the same sex. You're a lucky man."

Bertie stared at the ground. Then he said, without much enthusiasm, "Well, I suppose you'll be wanting to see the bails and dairy."

"Ah, yes," said, Mr Kissop, as though that suggestion was a surprising one.

"If you'd like a cup of tea . . . " suggested Bertie.

"A cup of tea," repeated the inspector; and Bertie's hopes rose a trifle. He regretted, mildly, and for the first time, that he was a teetotaller. Probably Mr Kissop, being a jovial man, was not.

Ted Kissop's eyebrows shot upwards when he entered the kitchen. There were fifteen cats inhabiting the chairs, the table and various half empty sacks of feed. Bertie, noting the surprise, hastened to explain.

"I keep that feed for the fowls," he said proudly. "That bag there's for the black chooks, and that over there for the Rhode Islands, and the other for the Leghorns. Keep a check on what they eat, and so I know my profits."

"Ah," said the inspector doubtfully. "A man with a system, eh, Mr Curtis?"

"In here," said Bertie, taking him into the storeroom, "are the bags for the pigs. They have a bag each."

"But you don't feed them in here," said Mr Kissop, shocked.

"Oh, no," said Bertie; "not on your life. But they try to get in, the little coots. I've caught 'em more than once at the wrong bags."

Mr Kissop allowed his gaze to fall lightly upon the fowls, of varied colours, pecking their way along the hallway. Bertie sighted them also, and divining that this was no place for fowls, or not today, anyway, rushed at them, spreading his arms. "Sh-hoo!" he said, his voice cracking as he endeavoured, vainly, to register indignation.

It was at this point Mr Kissop declined tea. No, he was firm about it. There were other farms to be seen, as Bertie well knew. Bertie later considered that it was at this point he had lost any advantage he might have had over the tall inspector.

Mr Kissop shook his head slowly when he surveyed the feed in the fourth bail. He pointed that out to Bertie, who quickly countered the suggestion with his fifteen cats "and some to come". Mr Kissop nodded doubtfully, and proceeded to the third bail, where he peered into feed-drums. He shook his head even more doubtfully. At the second bail he almost wept. There were a litter of machine-parts, tools, grease and oil. ''I see,'' he observed sadly, ''that you use only one bail, Mr Curtis.''

''Only one,'' said Bertie, brightening. ''They know just when they've got to come in, Inspector, and come in they do. Saves a lot of time.'' Bertie shook his head and said, ''I don't know why some go to all the trouble of bailing them up in different bails.''

Mr Kissop continued to look sad. ''No, I suppose you don't, Mr Curtis,'' was all he said.

It was true that the yards were spotlessly clean, cobbled and without manure. Bertie's large vegetable-garden received its portion daily, and so Mr Kissop was able to breathe freely on that score. But the dairy itself cancelled those few good marks. It was littered, too, with harness and pieces of metal-scrap, worn-out horseshoes, rusty cans and — the gods forgive Mr Curtis — drums of sour skim! Mr Kissop had ceased shaking his head. He was numbed it seemed and now expected anything.

''Those pigs you have, Mr Curtis,'' he said suddenly, ''where are they?''

''Oh, way out there,'' said Bertie, pointing towards the furthest reaches of his farm.

''Ah,'' said Mr Kissop. He seemed to breathe more freely.

Then it was he said the amazing words, the sentence which, then and when he had departed, burned and continued to burn deeply into the mind of the bachelor-dairyman.

''What you need, Mr Curtis,'' he had said, ''is to get yourself a wife.''

A
BID
FOR
BEAUTY

Not very big, Mr Gossip, not very big at all. Quite an ordinary man, Gus Gossip, but pleasant enough, advancing from his car, crossing the delightful sunlight.

"Hullo, Gus!" says one, and "G'day, Gus," says another, and so it may be seen that the whole assembly of men, women, sulkies, utility trucks, large trucks, cars and cattle-floats are all for Gus, or wish to appear so. It seems they have all more than a moment to nod towards Gus and his gold-topped, gold-tipped cane, his small red face, his prosperous little figure, his quick confident walk.

"A great day for the rogues!" shouts old Charley Skeers, and the crowd roar at Charley's sally, and Gus grins, grins as though he knows Charley does not mean that, really, and so everybody is put in good humour despite the tremendous hotness of the day, and despite the dryness of it, too.

Miss Muriel Deakin, it seems, has a pleasant enough smile for Gus, also, although she does not bring the whole battery of it to bear upon Gus, but camouflages it somewhat, turning her head on the side like an impertinent canary, curious to know what that man thinks about this woman. Big Jim Deakin, whose cows are to be sold by Gus, extends a hand, smiles warmly, nods, clenches Gus's fat fist, and then releases it.

"Hot day, Gus," he says, slowly moving his great head.

"Hot day, all right, Jim," says Gus, and to prove it he whips out a large white handkerchief, shakes it until it has fluttered loose, screws it into half a ball and, clenching it in his chubby fist, wipes his now beaded face. Miss Deakin observes all these actions with that half-curious half-knowing look that is peculiar to women who have nearly reached their forties without being married.

"Maybe it's too hot, eh, Gus?" says Jim. "Maybe they won't sell too well, eh?"

"They'll sell," says Gus. "Look at them all, the great crowd of them there. There must be some buyers amongst them."

Of course there are. Bill Bye, Denny James, Arnold McGrath, Tim Hootie, Tom Baldwin. His eyes continue to search amongst the collection of men and women, young men and girls, children, dogs and horses. He allows his lips to move as he recognises this one and that. He half smiles at times, and finally looks at Jim, gives a wink which is both devilish and joyous, and says that "they'll sell, all right".

Jim mutters relievedly, and proceeds to use his handkerchief. It seems Jim is more than a trifle nervous about the whole business. Gus knows that it comes hard to a man to have to sell his stock. He has a moment's feeling for Jim, and in that moment forgets he is an auctioneer.

"Wouldn't be selling, you know, Gus," says Jim, "if it wasn't for this damned side of mine."

Gus nods sympathetic agreement.

"Muriel here is a great help," says Jim, glancing at Muriel, "but you can't leave all the work to the young woman."

"No," says Gus meditatively, "you can't, Jim." He glances towards Muriel and gives her an intimate nod of recognition and appreciation.

"You won't be sorry, eh, Miss Muriel?" he says.

She shakes her head, but does not trust herself to speak. She hides that hungry look in her eyes.

Gus then becomes businesslike. He picks up the cane, which he has let dangle by his side. He grasps it firmly in the right hand, thrusts it determinedly forwards, so that it is a rigid rod. He pokes it upwards, half turns upon his heels, and says to Jim,

"We'll have a look over the stock before the sale starts, Boss,"
and Jim says it is a good idea because Gus can then know what
he is selling.

Miss Muriel watches them go, and her eyes are now very
admiring in expression as she watches the small, dapper
auctioneer walk away with her father. She also seems a trifle
wistful. Jim and Gus make towards the kikuyu paddock, the
only green patch in this dry brownness of pasture.

"Mind you," Gus is saying, "the prices mightn't be tops,
Jim. Most of the men on the River are overstocked. Some of
them were nearly cleaned out with the flood last autumn. You
didn't get it real bad here, you know. They had the winter to go
through on top of everything. If we don't get rain soon it'll be
another bad winter."

"I know. I know that, Gus," says Jim. "Still, if you can get
some sort of a price . . ."

"Keep 'em coming," says Gus, half shouting. "Keep 'em
coming all the time, Jim. Run 'em in, one after the other. Keep
'em coming. Don't let the sale lag. They'll sell, don't you
worry.

"Last week," says Gus, "had a sale at Broughton's down on
the Flats. What does he do, Broughton, but haggle and moan
over every cow. 'I want an extra quid of that one, Gus,' he says,
or, 'I couldn't let it go for that, Gus.' He's holding the line of
them up all the time and everyone's getting tired, especially of
his whinging face. No, Jim, keep 'em coming and don't
quibble."

He draws the gold-tipped, gold-topped cane through his
hands, passes it backwards and forwards, held high, across his
chest. "Tell you what, Jim," he says. "I got a letter from the
brother this week. Know what they are fetching down the South
Coast, in the Valley? Good stock, mind you, like yours.
Fifty-two pounds ten! Hard to believe, I know. Could hardly
believe it myself, but there it is, the brother got that for one
cow."

140

"Good cows, eh?" says Jim, only half believing what he hears.

They are now looking at Jim's stock and Gus raises a protest. "No better'n yours, Jim, I'll bet," he cries. "Your stuff is the best up this way. No better on the River."

"Not enough water here, Gus," says Jim sadly. "Now, if it hadn't been for this side of mine . . ."

Gus nods sympathetically. "It's a bad thing, that side of yours," he says. He points to a well-conditioned mature Jersey dam. "Fine beast that, Jim," he says.

"Best in the herd," says Jim, his eyes glowing. He is beginning to be stud master. "Reared her myself," he says. "At least, Muriel did. She had it for a pet.Calf out of a good pedigreed cow I bought. Good bull, the father. Calf better than the mother. No calf now of course."

Gus nods. He runs a practised eye over the whole herd, lets his gaze slip up and down, across and sideways about the full-bellied cows, the dainty slim-legged heifers, the nuggety calves, the solid bulls. He sighs for the stock, which must go cheaply, too cheaply because of the weather.

"I'll do my best, Jim," he says solemnly, and he means it.

He is sure he means it when next he sees Miss Muriel. He has a keen look this time, and is glad she is just that trifle distant, that fraction cool towards him, and all the time, over and over in his mind, he turns a picture of last night when he visited old Sam Foster his bachelor neighbour. Dirty old man, Sam, with dirty stubbled face, and dirty fingers, cutting bread on a table covered with years of crumbs and succeeding layers of newspapers. One end of it a few dirty tins, some partly filled with jam, some empty, and the jam gone hard about the edges. Flies on the table, and flies on the ceiling, and flies where Sam had swept, year after year, his rubbish into one corner.

Gus was sure he would never come to that, but seeing Miss Muriel made him think how much easier she might make it for him, keeping neat and dapper, with an occasional rub of the chamois for his gold tipped-topped cane. It is as though Gus sees the writing on the wall, and then, at the sight of Miss Muriel, there is a blast of trumpets about his head, a silver clashing of cymbals, a belting upon the timbrels. All this at the sight of her standing amidst the piles of sandwiches and the large white teapots.

But there is the sale, and Gus must not hesitate, so that he swings his stick as he walks, all the time keeping one eye open for Jerry and the boys. Jerry is his aged clerk, his grizzled offsider, so alert that he never misses a bid, and is always ready with his "yes," shouted so that no one is in doubt that he has a bid. Jack is a sort of offsider, and is responsible for bringing in each beast, and hunting out the animal sold, that Gus may keep attention fixed upon the animal being auctioned.

There are others, too, all indispensable to Gus, for they keep up a running of noise, a nodding and a shouting so that there is never doubt about the sale being a lively one, and there is always a helpful bid or two, cunningly interposed when the selling might otherwise slacken.

Today, however, Gus feels the sale is somehow different. He remembers the letter from brother George, and the price George managed to get for a cow. Then there is Miss Muriel, old Sam, and the best cow in the herd. He opens the gate, walks in, closely followed by grizzled Jerry, Jack and the boys.

The cows are driven from the kikuyu paddock to the stockyard. The stockyard is divided, and Gus uses one portion for selling. He says a word to Jerry, who then walks across to Jack. Jack speaks to the boys, and a cow is run into the selling yard. It is any sort of a cow, to be truthful, but it has the effect of stopping some of the talking that goes on about the rails.

Gus then puts up his arms. He spreads wide the fat fingers of his hands. He commands silence. He is about to say something. Old-timers look away as though they, of all people, are not interested in this sale. One or two buyers try to catch Gus's eye, but fail. The little auctioneer stands, arms upwards, cane leaning against his right thigh.

"I am about to declare this sale on," he says. "I am about to declare the sale on. I am selling today on behalf of Mr Jim Deakin. You all know Jim. Jim's putting up all his stock, without reserve. You know the rule — everything to the highest bidder. Knocked down to the highest bidder. Terms strictly cash unless otherwise arranged. Good, well she's on.''

And she is on. Gus makes a grab at his cane, swishes it at the cow which is before him, looks at it in a surprised manner, and says to Jerry. ''A milking cow, Jerry, that's what we want.''

Well then, the dry cow is run out, and a milker run in, one calved the day before, its calf bawling at its side, its udder swaying bulbously. The cow is an exceptionally good one, and so Gus appeals.

''Now what am I offered for this fine beast. Good as you'll see anywhere on the River. Now come on, who'll start her off at a tenner?''

No one will start her off at a tenner. Gus is disgusted. ''Tell you what,'' he says, magnanimously, ''I'll start her at eight quid. A gift. Who'll give me eight quid for this cow.''

Eight quid it is. Eight pound ten. Nine pounds. No more bids.

''Come on. Come on,'' says Gus with surprise. ''No advance on nine? Any advance on nine pounds? Yes, nine pounds ten to you. Ten pounds. Any advance on ten pounds?''

''Yes!'' shouts Jerry. ''Yes!'' shouts Jack. ''Yes!'' all the boys shout, and the sale moves on merrily, but stops at twelve pounds.

Gus shakes his head sadly. ''What?'' he says. ''Only twelve pounds for this beautiful beast. Come on, she'll pay for herself in a month. Pound of butter a day, easily.''

Twelve pounds ten. Then fourteen pounds and Gus has set the sale. No more milking cows at this juncture. Gus looks disappointed, as though the cow is being given away. He looks at big Jim. ''What about it, Jim?'' he asks; ''will you let it go?''

''Let her go,'' says Jim heartily. Magnanimous Jim. Jim can't believe he got that price at all. He tries not to appear pleased.

''Keep 'em coming,'' says Gus, ''keep 'em coming.''

Well, they keep them coming, heifers this time, the first one a slim-legged beauty, just springing. Gus runs up the price. Heifers will fetch more than milkers.

"All their life ahead of them," Gus tells the farmers, who know that, anyway.

So the sale is on. Gus and the boys catch the bids, shoot up the prices, and Jim, watching, continues to be magnanimous. There is no let-up, the stock being pushed from one yard to another. Everyone fancies there must be wads of money about, and that it is the right thing to buy stock now, even if the weather is dry, even if the grass is eaten out, even though there may be another poor winter ahead. Good stock always sell well, and Jim has only good stock.

Miss Muriel watches, peering between the split rails, and Gus catches sight of her, so that there is quite an amount of cane work, a twisting of it in his fingers, a glistening and glittering of top and ferrule in the sun. Gus will not let the stock go cheaply, although he avows it is what he is doing.

There is a sudden lag in the bidding. Gus can almost hear the sigh from the crowd. "You cockies always like an early lunch," he says. "All right then, you know where the pear tree is."

Of course they know where the pear tree is. They also know the large white teapots, and the huge piles of sandwiches. Some work towards the china-pear from the barn way, others go straight to the food, but all seem to converge at the point, about the same time.

There is an exchange of greetings, and a grabbing of cups, taking of sandwiches, and endeavours to be served with tea, sugar and, should you like it, milk. There is a gabbling and a talking, a swelling of sound as the whole district of Coolbucca gets down to some steady gossiping.

Muriel it is who gets Gus his cup, and that is right and proper, and Gus is grateful. He watches Muriel pouring tea, daintily, and he thinks of old Sam, and the jam-tins on the table. Nothing

144

of this shows in his eyes, and Miss Muriel, of course, is a trifle distant, as usual.

However, she does say, with some enthusiasm. "I think you did marvellously, Mr Gossip. You seemed to be quite disappointed. I'm sure father was really pleased with the prices."

"You do?" says Gus. He seemed pleased also. He smiles. "To tell the truth, Miss Muriel," he says, "I'm pleased too. It is a good sale."

He looks at big Jim's daughter. "Wait!" he says in a fairly impressive voice. "Wait until this afternoon."

"Oh?" says Miss Muriel, delicate query in her voice.

"Wait," says Gus, "till we sell that good cow. You know, the one you reared."

"Beauty," says Miss Muriel, quick as a flash. "Well, I do hope you get a good price for her, Mr Gossip."

"M'm," says Gus. He wishes, somehow, she would not call him "Mister".

When the crops are discussed, the condition of the cows upon the River, the murder up at Two Stones Creek, the Show moved into Reg Brown's old place ("funny ideas you know"), then there is time left for the remainder of the sale, and Gus leads the way, his cane swinging at his side, and as Gus goes he looks at the sky, which is faintly smudged with cloud, and when he has the yard as his stage again, and the crowded fence as his audience, he raises his cane, pointing it towards the smudge, and says, "Rain, boys. You'll have to bid quick if you don't want to be drenched."

The boys laugh at this, for they have almost forgotten what rain is, and someone says, "What's rain, Gus?" and there is a general laugh at that, and Gus laughs too, and when someone says, "Might be another flood, Gus," the whole crowd is in good humour, and because its communal stomach is fed there is general goodwill and a fine opportunity for high bids.

The buyers, however, are still cautious, and Gus has to encourage them. Jim lets the cows go at whatever the buyers want to pay for them, and Gus tells Jerry and the boys to keep them coming, and when there are only a few left, then Gus walks across to Jerry, whispering something to him, and Jerry whispers to Jack, and Jack goes away, and finally, after selling a cow or two, Gus nods to Jack, and says, ''Bring her in, Jack.'' This in the tone of a proud ringmaster about to display his best lion.

To tell the truth there has been a grub in Gus's mind, a small persistent grub, one that has wriggled and wriggled, finally lying dormant chrysalising, de-chrysalising, and becoming a beautiful butterfly. Gus knows it has everything to do with Muriel, and she, infatuated girl, is still peering through the fence at Gus.

''Bring her in,'' says Gus, and they bring her in, not pushing her forwards, not shouting at her, or twisting her tail, thumping her upon the rump, but actually leading her, a halter on her head, her horns gleaming because they are polished, her hocks and hooves shining because they have been scraped, and her whole coat glistening because she has been well groomed.

She takes every eye. Her udder bellies, her milk veins stand out, her back is straight as a ruler, her head held high. Gus, looking at her, thinks he will surely write to brother George and tell what he got for this cow. That is the thought which once was a grub, which now is a butterfly, a confused symbol of high prices, Miss Muriel and Gus, all crowded together, all the one thing.

''Now,'' says Gus heavily, and breathing hard, because he is a little excited. ''We have here the best cow on the River, bar none.'' It does not matter that they are not quite on the River. Everyone knows what Gus means, and some nod, and none dares deny the truth.

''Absolutely the best cow,'' says Gus firmly. He looks about. His cane is held, shoulder height, at the horizontal. It points at the crowd.

''I am not going to call for a bid,'' says Gus. ''I'm starting the bidding myself, at thirty pounds.''

Gus Gossip is starting the bidding at thirty pounds. Gus

Gossip might buy the cow himself. Gus Gossip is offering the highest price for a cow this season.

"Thirty pounds," says Gus solemnly. "Any advance on thirty pounds?"

Miss Muriel is no longer haughty. Some sort of adoration shines from her eyes, and Gus sees that, but he keeps his mind on the matter in hand, and asks again, of the silent crowd, whether there is any advance on thirty pounds.

The silence is broken. "Yes!" shouts Jerry. "Yes!" shouts Jack. "Yes!" say all the boys. It is "Yes" all the time, a chorus of yesses as the buyers compete. Thirty pounds is thirty-five pounds. No ten-shilling bids here. Thirty-five pounds is forty pounds. Is forty-two pounds, forty-three pounds. It is forty-six pounds, and then no bidding.

"You won't believe it, Gus," brother George had written. "But I got fifty-two pounds ten for a cow this week." The butterfly hovers in Gus's mind. He will not look at the fence.

"Any advance on forty-six pounds?" he asks. There is no response. "I'll have to knock it down to the highest bidder," he threatens, and the suspense-sick buyers break, and away the bidding goes again, although this time in ten-shillings. Gus follows it up, helps to push it, holds the same dread threat over the heads of the bidders, and the cow is at fifty pounds.

Gus, looking at Miss Muriel, is alarmed to see her shaking her head in a negative sort of gesture. It seems almost to roll, as though she were having a fit.

Gus has a fearful feeling, suddenly, that she does not wish him to sell the beast, and with that feeling is alarm at the terrific price the cow is fetching.

Is there something wrong with it? he is inclined to ask himself, but the cow is there, for all to see, and the buyers all want it. He tears his fascinated gaze away from the shaking head, forgets his feelings for Miss Muriel and proceeds to flog the bidding. He holds the threat over the heads of the buyers, the threat of knocking it down, and the bidding has a last spurt which brings it to fifty-two pounds, and there it stays and will not budge. Mr Denis James, from Belmont on the River, has bid a record price for a cow.

Gus holds his hands up, his cane clenched in his right fist. He pivots, looking at the crowd. He would dearly like to write to George, and tell him about getting fifty-two pounds ten, or fifty-three pounds for a cow, but the silent crowd eye him, and will not bid. "I am going to knock this fine cow down to the highest bidder," says Gus, his cane turning with his slow pivoting.

Gus knocks it down. His cane falls, lies limply in his hands. Gus says to Jerry, "Put that down to Mr James, Jerry," and Jerry puts it down to Mr James, and Jack dabs some blue paint on the glistening rump.

The sale, then, is as good as over. The last few head of stock are passed through, fetch ordinary prices, almost amid silence. When the last cow is daubed blue it is the signal for an outbreak of chattering, a rumbling of comments and questions, a deluge of conversation.

Big Jim bears down upon Gus and takes his hand, pumps it hard, slaps Gus on the back, and declares he just can't believe it. Gus says he can't either, if it comes to that, and as soon as he can get away from Jim he does. Jim, restless now, wanders off, and Miss Muriel hurries up to the little auctioneer. Her eyes are shining, her aloofness has gone. She has a light in her eyes.

"You were wonderful, Gus," she exclaims, not noticing she has forgotten his surname.

"You think so, Miss Muriel?" he says, surprised. "I thought you didn't want me to sell your cow at that price."

"It's Dad's cow," she says. "And I did want to sell it at that price. Why, it was wonderful!"

A little butterfly raises its battered wings and prepares to fly.

"I wanted to get fifty-two pounds ten, or fifty-three pounds for that cow," says Gus.

"Why ever?" laughs Miss Muriel, amazed. "That was a wonderful price."

Gus realises, then, that Miss Muriel would not understand, not knowing about brother George, down the south coast.

"It's like this, Miss Muriel," he says earnestly.

"Muriel," she corrects him, with a nervous giggle.

Gus's butterfly prepares for flight. "It's like this, Muriel," he says.